Irrigation and Agricultural Politics in South Korea

Westview Replica Editions

This book is a Westview Replica Edition. The concept of Replica Editions is a response to the crisis in academic and informational publishing. Library budgets for books have been severely curtailed; economic pressures on the university presses and the few private publishing companies primarily interested in scholarly manuscripts have severely limited the capacity of the industry to properly serve the academic and research communities. Many manuscripts dealing with important subjects, often representing the highest level of scholarship, are today not economically viable publishing projects. Or, if they are accepted for publication, they are often subject to lead times ranging from one to three years. Scholars are understandably frustrated when they realize that their first-class research cannot be published within a reasonable time frame, if at all.

Westview Replica Editions are our practical solution to the problem. The concept is simple. We accept a manuscript in camera-ready form and move it immediately into the production process. The responsibility for textual and copy editing lies with the author or sponsoring organization. If necessary we will advise the author on proper preparation of footnotes and bibliography. We prefer that the manuscript be typed according to our specifications, though it may be acceptable as typed for a dissertation or prepared in some other clearly organized and readable way. The end result is a book produced by lithography and bound in hard covers. Initial edition sizes range from 400 to 800 copies, and a number of recent Replicas are already in second printings. We include among Westview Replica Editions only works of outstanding scholarly quality or of great informational value, and we will continue to exercise our usual editorial standards and quality control.

About the Book and Author

Irrigation and Agricultural Politics in South Korea

Robert Wade

Studies of the role of irrigation in agricultural development generally focus on the amount of land under irrigation, the cost of irrigation, the physical structures for irrigation, etc. In this book the author takes a different perspective, examining how state and local institutions that manage water conveyance and drainage actually function. He thus reveals a great deal about the relationships and power struggles that exist between government and the people and between central and local authorities.

The case used in this study is South Korea, a developing country experiencing a consistent, rapid increase in its GNP and one of the few that has chosen the capitalist, rather than socialist, route to development. By examining the ongoing debate about the superiority of one or the other ideology in the development efforts of LDCs, the author links the specific issues of irrigation management to the larger issues of the role of the state in South Korean development. How does the central government control the countryside, and how do local agents and country dwellers react to attempts at control? Dr. Wade concludes that the authoritarian and pervasively interventionist nature of its government has contributed to South Korea's successful approach to economic development.

Robert Wade has been a fellow of the Institute of Development Studies, University of Sussex, since 1972. He has published articles on a variety of topics in rural development, including administrative and political aspects of irrigation in India, South Korea, and Italy.

Irrigation and Agricultural Politics in South Korea

Robert Wade

Westview Press / Boulder, Colorado

Published in 1982 in the United States of America by
    Westview Press, Inc.
    5500 Central Avenue
    Boulder, Colorado 80301
    Frederick A. Praeger, Publisher

Library of Congress Catalog Card Number: 81-19704
ISBN: 0-86531-264-8

Printed and bound in the United States of America

To Susan Joekes, companion-in-arms;
for my parents, Hunter and Avelda Wade;
and with respect to Frank Holmes,
Professor of Economics, who taught that
the political and social often dominate
the economic.

Contents

Tables and Figures

Preface

Economic analyses of the role of irrigation in agricultural development normally measure 'irrigation' in terms of the proportion of total cultivated land which is irrigated (the adequacy and reliability of the irrigation being taken for granted), or in terms of investment cost, or in terms of the density of physical structures (metres of field channel per hectare, for example). Conspicuously missing from the irrigation literature are studies of how the institutions for water conveyance and drainage actually work, especially where those institutions are part of the government bureaucracy rather than autonomous 'communal' bodies. Yet the adequacy and reliability of water supply to farmers' fields depends on how these institutions work. To understand better the impact of 'irrigation' on yields, total production, employment, and innovation we need to understand irrigation management institutions. This essay is about the irrigation management institutions of South Korea.

At the same time it is also about state control of the populace. Irrigation canals above a rather small size are in most countries operated by government departments or parastatal agencies, whose procedures and operations are shaped by and form part of the wider structure of local and state-level power. Irrigation organisation is a way into the study of more general questions about the links between government and populace, between central government and local government. That the context of this study is South Korea, which has experienced an extraordinarily rapid rate of growth of GNP over the 1960s and most of the 1970s, gives these questions a particular interest. We know that the South Korean government has been both authoritarian and pervasively interventionist in economic and other spheres. But there are few detailed studies of how the bureaucratic apparatus works; and on questions of how the central government controls its local agents, how those local agents control the countryside, and the reaction of both local agents and country dwellers to attempts at control

from above - the literature is distinctly meagre.
Irrigation organisation is a path to these questions.
And further, the tendencies in the wider field of power
have an important effect on how the irrigation
organisations themselves operate, and hence on the link
between irrigation and yields, employment, and other
such 'economic' variables. In this immediately obvious
sense, politics and economics are closely interlinked,
and to study the economics of irrigation without the
politics is to miss many of the critical issues.

In 1978 I was asked by the International Labour
Organisation's Team for Employment Promotion in Asia
(ARTEP) to make a study of irrigation organisation in
an East Asian country, following my earlier research on
the same subject in India. Taiwan might well have
been chosen, for enough is known about its irrigation
institutions to suggest that they are by international
comparison very effective, although no detailed studies
of the behaviour, relationships, and purposes of those
who operate the institutions have been made. But
Taiwan was ruled out by its exclusion from the United
Nations, which means that no UN funds (including mine)
can be spent there. Japan seemed unsuitable because
its irrigation institutions would probably be heavily
affected in their operation and physical equipment by
the very high capitalisation of agriculture which has
taken place in the past two decades; its present-day
patterns would therefore be even further removed from
the conditions of South and Southeast Asia than those
of the other two cases. Of the 'mixed' economies of
East Asia, South Korea was left.

I carried out field work in South Korea for 12 weeks
between June and September 1979. Most of the time was
spent studying one particular Farmland Improvement
Association, said to be one of the best-run in South Korea.
My research assistant and I lived in the small town
where the headquarters of the Association is located and
spent each day with staff of the Association (or related
government offices), and with farmers. I also made
brief visits to several other parts of South Korea, and a
short private visit to Taiwan, spent in the area of the
Chianan Irrigation Association. I moved freely in
South Korea, without government supervision, and the
choice of the Farmland Improvement Association was
entirely mine. On the other hand, most, but not all,
of the farmers I spoke to at length were suggested by
officials of the Association, though the officials were
never present, and it turned out that some of these
same nominated farmers were highly (if guardedly)
critical of the Association. The research was conducted
before the assassination of President Park Chung-hee,
and when I refer to the present government, I mean Park's.

K.N. Raj, while head of ARTEP, suggested the study, and Wilbert Gooneratne of ARTEP facilitated arrangements. My official host in South Korea was the Korea Rural Economics Institute. To its Research Director, Dr. In-Joung Whang, and to Dr. Oh Ho-Sung, Fellow in Natural Resources, my sincere thanks for their help. The field work was made easier in many and varied ways by Alan McBain of UNICEF, Ken and Marjory Cunningham of the New Zealand Embassy, Chang-Nak Choi, and especially Tony and Pilwah Michell. Su Young Chan, my interpreter and research assistant, contributed insight, diligence and good cheer. The staff of SY Farmland Improvement Association displayed extraordinary patience in answering questions without end.

To two colleagues at the Institute of Development Studies I owe a particular debt - Manfred Bienefeld, from whom I have learned much about the significance of South Korea for the wider development debate, and Ronald Dore, from whom I have learned about Confucian societies and much else besides. Dore read Chapters 2 to 6 in draft and made characteristically useful comments.

Because the essay is in some ways critical of South Korea's irrigation institutions and the structure of power in which they operate, it is particularly necessary, given the political complexion of the country and the understandable desire of its government officials to see South Korea presented as a model for other countries, to make clear that none of these people bear any responsibility for what follows; that is mine alone.

Susan Saunders typed the first draft; Jacky Kulkarni, assisted by Susan Fasquelle, prepared it for camera-ready copy. Rebecca Smith did the index. I acknowledge their help with thanks.

NOTE

In 1979 the exchange rate was about 500 won to the US dollar.

Irrigation and Agricultural
Politics in South Korea

1
State Control and Irrigation

> Only by moving grandly on the macroscopic
> level can we satisfy our intellectual and human
> curiosities. But only by moving minutely on
> the molecular level can our observations and
> explanations be adequately connected. So, if
> we would have our cake and eat it too, we must
> shuttle between macroscopic and molecular
> levels in instituting the problem and in
> explaining it (Mills 1963, p. 563).

THE WIDER SIGNIFICANCE OF THE SOUTH KOREAN CASE

The broad indicators of South Korea's economic
growth from the early 1960s to the mid 1970s are
among the best known statistics in the development
literature: from 1965 to 1975, Gross National
Product grew at an average annual rate of 10 percent
(in constant prices), value added in manufacturing
at 20 percent, and total exports at an exploding 31
percent. This gives the country one of the best
sustained, non natural-resource-dependent growth
records of any in the Third World. Moreover, rapid
growth in GNP has created a labour shortage, causing
impressive increases in real wages; mass consumption
levels have increased dramatically, and income
distribution by social class has remained relatively
equal compared to most other non-socialist Third
World countries. [1]
When slow economic growth, increasing inequality
and even absolute deterioration in living conditions
for the poorest fifth of the population is the much
more typical experience of Third World countries, it
is not surprising that South Korea's avowedly
capitalist growth has given rise to strongly contrasted and passionately defended interpretations.
Ultimately the issue at stake is the superiority of

1

the capitalist or the socialist way to development -
and indeed, the meanings to be given to these terms.
For some, South Korea, together with Taiwan, Hong
Kong and Singapore, constitute the 'East Asian'
model of successful capitalist development in the
post-Second World War period. They vindicate the
prescription of neo-classical economics, that the
government's chief role should be limited to keeping
markets free, or by means of incentive policies
ensuring those prices which would have prevailed if
markets had been free of 'distortions'. Today's
less developed countries, wanting a development route
which will combine rapid growth without rapidly
increasing inequality, are advised to follow the
East Asian model, on the assumption that what is
possible is replicable.

For others, however, South Korea's 'success'
is the result of the exploitation of cheap Korean
labour by Japanese and United States capital, and
will continue only for as long as the cost of
labour is kept below that of emerging competitors.
The government's chief role, it is argued, has been
to control labour and prevent overt unrest by means
of brutal repression. South Korea is a 'house built
on sand', a 'tottering neo-colony'; it in no way
refutes the proposition that only a socialist form
of development will prove viable in the longer run.[2]

Stated so briefly, these characterisations are
necessarily overdrawn. Yet it is important to
realise how potent the South Korean experience is
taken to be for supporting and casting doubt upon
basic ideological positions in current development
debates.

The question of the validity of the interpretations is therefore one whose interest extends
well beyond the particular. Both interpretations,
I suggest, have serious weaknesses. The free
market view underestimates the significance of a
combination of two features of the 'international
environment' in which South Korea's industrialisation
took place: the availability of massive loan funds
from the industrial economies; and easy access
for labour-intensive manufactures into industrial
country markets. To go into the details of this
international context and how it has changed in the
1970s would be a digression; suffice it to say here
(we return to the issue briefly in Chapter 8) that
this combination no longer exists to anything like
the same degree as in the 1960s, which seems to make
South Korea much less relevant a model for underdeveloped countries today. Secondly, the free

market view glosses over the repression, the
violation of civil rights and political freedoms,
the emasculation of trade unions, which accompanied
the industrialisation drive, helping to keep the
labour market free, and to assure foreign lenders
of their loans and domestic investors of their
profits. [3]

On the other hand, the second view ignores
evidence that while South Korea may have begun its
export growth as a cheap labour annex of Japan and
the United States - and so with its economic growth
'at the invitation of' those countries [4] - it had,
by the 1970s at least, reached a position of being
able to use foreign loan and investment capital on
its own terms, rather than being used by it. South
Korea has reached this position because it has been
able to implement policies defined in terms of
national long-run objectives (often against the
advice of international lending agencies like the
World Bank). [5] In the light of evidence on the
growth of the country's chemical, heavy and
technology-intensive industries, the cruder versions
of 'dependency theory', which say that close
integration with the world economy renders a viable
industrialisation virtually impossible, clearly
require a good deal of qualification. [6]

Moreover, both views make the mistake of
treating South Korea as among the most 'capitalist'
of less developed economies, in line with the image
which the South Korean government itself presents
of the country for the purpose of differentiating
it as sharply as possible from North Korea. Both
views underestimate the extent to which the state has
been actively and pervasively interventionist in
industry and in agriculture, through instruments of
discretionary command as well as through the market;
and as part of this intervention, has limited and
directed the power of accumulation of private
capital, in both industry and agriculture. By the
early 1970s, the government directly or indirectly
controlled the allocation of more than two thirds
of the investment fund of the economy - a level of
control over investment which few states outside
the socialist bloc have come near to matching. [7]

While the broad importance of command is
reasonably clear to any student of South Korea who
spends more than a short time in the country and is
not concerned primarily to vindicate neo-classical
economics, research on how the South Korean government has actually implemented its policies, with
what blend of command and market, through what

bureaucratic decision-structures, is surprisingly
thin, given the huge literature on the South
Korean case. [8]   The first group tends to avoid the
question by assuming that 'policies explain growth'
(so this literature tends to be long on congratulatory
description of what the policies - especially the
trade policies - were, and even longer on statistics
about the 'outcomes'); while the second, 'anti'
group, is inclined to be impatient of detailed
analysis of implementation, except perhaps insofar
as implementation shows the mechanism of repression
in action.
    This study is about the methods and organisation
of state intervention in the field of agriculture
generally, irrigation specifically.

AGRICULTURAL POLITICS

    The question of how the rural population has
been controlled and rendered 'stable' is important
for understanding South Korea's development path.
Undoubtedly, the land reform of the late 1940s and
early 1950s removed one major cause of unrest in the
countryside, thereby allowing the post Second World
War regimes to concentrate their repressive apparatus
on the cities; and the Korean War of the early
1950s resulted in an unusual homogeneity of ideological persuasion in the country at large, as left-
wing partisans either moved to North Korea or were
killed off. But how is it that unrest in the
countryside has been prevented from spreading,
becoming organised, in the intervening period,
especially during the 1960s when the terms of trade
between countryside and city, agriculture and
industry, were turned hard against the countryside
to provide a surplus for investment in industry?
    The question of how South Korean farmers have
become as productive as they are is also important
for understanding South Korea's development. While
it is true that agriculture has been less important
in sustaining industrialisation than it would have
been if large flows of cheap food imports had not
been available, it is also true that agriculture
did, especially through compulsory food procurement
in the 1950s and 1960s, make an important
contribution to South Korean industrialisation and
that its high and rising levels of productivity per
hectare facilitated this contribution. South Korea
now boasts the highest rice yields per hectare in
the world. Granted that the reason has something
to do with high levels of manufactured inputs, how

has the government forced, cajoled or encouraged
farmers to adopt these high levels?
     The answers to these two leading questions -
about the 'stability' of the countryside, and
high agricultural productivity - have to do with
the way the state has manipulated a complex spectrum
of economic and coercive sanctions in order to
enforce and facilitate its orders and procedures.
The agriculture of South Korea, like its industry,
has been thoroughly embraced by the state. While
it is true that its agriculture is based on small
scale family farms (average cultivated area per farm
household is only about one hectare), there is a
sense in which the whole country might be described
as 'one' farm, so small is the residual area of
farmers' free decision-making left over by the
tightly controlled large-scale context. [9]
     The 'one farm' image seems at first sight to
have affinities with the broad thrust of Marx's
argument on the 'Asiatic mode of production' and of
Wittfogel's 'Oriental despotism'. [10]   Both writers
emphasise the significance of control over water, and
specifically the construction, maintenance and
operation of irrigation canals, for providing
conditions prompting the growth of a certain form of
despotic political regime.   The argument has not
stood up well to theoretical or empirical examination, [11] however, and it is especially weak in
the context of South Korea.
     State control over irrigation water is not a
vital factor in the politics of South Korea; whereas state control over other agricultural inputs,
such as credit and fertiliser, is indeed very
important as a means of control over the rural
population.   For one thing, irrigation water is
generally in ample supply in relation to demand.
For another, water is not divisible in the same way
that credit, seeds and fertiliser are, in the sense
that it is difficult for the supplier to discriminate
between individual irrigators but not difficult for
the supplier to discriminate between individual
applicants for the other inputs.   Finally, most
irrigation systems in South Korea are small in scale
(less than 50 hectares of irrigated area), too
small and numerous for the state to control their
operation in any detail.
     In this book, therefore, irrigation is treated
not as a determining influence on local and national
politics (in the Wittfogelian or Marxian manner),
but as a specific context in which to examine
the operation of state power and policies.

Irrigation in South Korea means rice; rice is the
staple foodgrain, most farmers grow some, and most
rice is irrigated. In dealing with 'irrigators'
one is therefore dealing with the bulk of the
farming population. Most irrigation systems are
small-scale, however, and these, as noted, are
relatively independent of state control. Our focus
here is on the minority of systems irrigating
about 36 percent of South Korea's 1.1 million
hectares of irrigated land, which are bigger than
50 hectares and which therefore come under the
jurisdiction of a Farmland Improvement Association
(FLIA).

Farmland Improvement Associations are parastatal bodies, set up by and responsible to the
Ministry of Agriculture. Their job is to operate
and maintain (generally not construct) systems
above 50 hectares, to improve paddy land under the
systems, to give agricultural advice, and to cover
costs by collecting charges from the beneficiaries.
There are 122 FLIAs in the country as a whole, of
which three quarters have an irrigated area greater
than 500 hectares and less than 5,000 hectares.
They are the South Korean version of Japan's or
Taiwan's Irrigation Associations.

We shall be concerned with irrigation policies
specifically, agricultural policies more generally,
with the methods used to implement those policies,
and with the response of farmers to policies and
methods. We shall also be concerned with the
structure and operation of FLIAs, treated as one
type of agency of state intervention, as one of
several organisations on which large numbers of
rural South Koreans depend and are to some degree
and by various means controlled. It is true that
the FLIAs are not, for reasons already suggested,
amongst the most powerful levers of control over the
countryside; but they are nevertheless part of a
larger apparatus of control, and their internal
functioning and their relations with irrigators are,
as we shall see, strongly conditioned by this fact.

To be part of a larger apparatus of control,
however, does not mean that there are no serious
conflicts of interest between FLIAs and the central
government offices to which they are responsible.
The notion of a tightly-controlled large-scale state
embracing small-scale agriculture is indeed
potentially misleading if it is taken to imply a
more or less monolithic, conflict-free structure of
control of 'the people' by 'the government'. In
agriculture (more than in industry), many of the

goods and services provided by the state,
including monopoly supply of institutional credit,
fertiliser, and water (in the case of FLIA
irrigation systems), are provided not by lower
offices of the central government hierarchy but
by parastatal agencies which have some autonomy
both in principle and in practice.

But the autonomy is not simply conferred upon
them; it is, certainly in the case of the FLIAs and
probably in that of the others as well, a matter
which is continually fought over, and the operation
of the FLIAs, I shall show, cannot be understood
without recognising that defence of their own
interests against the control attempts of central
government is a dominant concern of the FLIA staff,
to which they give a good deal more attention than
they give the delivery of water and the maintenance
of the canals. The study of the FLIAs thus helps
to break down the idea of a simple impetus towards
control and repression of 'the people' by 'the state'
The questions we must address are how the central
government attempts to control its local parastatals
(in the case of the FLIAs), what is the response of
the FLIA staff to these attempts, and how well
central government controls ensure that the FLIAs
do their irrigation and agricultural work effectively?

In other words, the rural parastatals, because
relatively distant (in an administrative sense) from
central government control, are a particularly
interesting context in which to examine just how
effectively the state is able to implement orders
at its lower, rural levels. Furthermore, the
staff tend to be drawn from the area they work in,
and from the same broad social class as most of the
farmers; to what extent does this tend to moderate
their use of the more coercive techniques of obtaining obedience, or to soften the exclusion of farmers
from any influence on their decisions? And what
effects does their autonomy have on the care and
attention they give to those aspects of their
irrigation and agricultural work which are difficult
to supervise from the outside?

Both central government-FLIA and FLIA-farmer
relations, then, are to be the subject.

IRRIGATION INSTITUTIONS IN COMPARATIVE PERSPECTIVE

If irrigation provides a specific context in
which to study the details of state control in
South Korea, it is also of considerable interest in

its own right as a standard and major component in agricultural development budgets throughout the tropics. 'Irrigation and water management', indeed, is enjoying a fashion in development planning circles and international agencies; the Brandt Commission, for example, identifies it as the biggest single category of required investment in Third World agriculture. [12] One reason for such attention is that while the potential gains from the introduction of irrigation are typically very large, the actual performance of gravity-flow canal systems [13] in the tropics (on which the bulk of irrigation investment has been and will be spent) has tended to be poor. [14] Planners have often been dismayed that their plans, however carefully formulated, bear little relation to actual performance. The conventional assumption is that the causes of poor performance are primarily technical - to do with the physical structures for water delivery and drainage, or the state of land development, or the state of knowledge about crop-water-soil relationships. So a recent report to the Trilateral Commission estimates that rice production in South and Southeast Asia can be doubled in the 15 years between 1978 and 1993 if some $US 15 billion is spent on constructing field channels below the canal outlets of existing systems, on the assumption that insufficiency of field channels is a very important reason for poor performance. [15] To the extent that non-technical factors are considered relevant they are thought to pertain to what happens below the outlet, in the structure of social relations between irrigators.

However, recently a new discussion has been developing which poses as an issue, 'How much of the poor performance of canal irrigation can be attributed to the technical factors, and how much to bad management?' The answer, no doubt, is 'some of both', but there is a growing suspicion, particularly amongst social scientists, who have only recently begun to concern themselves with the management aspects of irrigated agriculture, that the conventional remedies are based on a very incomplete understanding of the processes involved on the institutional side, and therefore contain an inbuilt 'technological bias'. [16] This can be only part of the explanation of the technological bias, for it leaves out, amongst other things, the interests of many firms, governments, and international agencies in the huge flow of funds which that bias promotes. Nevertheless, it is certainly true that very little is known about management aspects of irrigated agriculture; studies of irrigation bureaucracies running large-scale (not communal) systems are conspicuous by their absence, for anywhere in Asia. 17   Levine's proposition, that 'Our knowledge of the interrelationships between water and plant growth far exceeds our knowledge of the interrelations between water and the human element in delivery and utilisation' (1977, p. 38), is eminently plausible.

The literature on Japan and Taiwan has emphasised the importance for understanding the performance of their irrigated agriculture of the particular institutional form through which irrigation canals have been constructed and operated. The Irrigation Associations bring together farmers under the same irrigation system to organise and operate it themselves, employing staff who(at least in principle) are responsible to farmers' representatives, and dividing up the operating and maintenance expenses between themselves. Such a form provides for effective liaison between staff and farmers, and disciplines the staff to operate the system effectively through the mechanisms of accountability of staff to farmers. This type of organisation was already well developed in Japan by the time it incorporated Taiwan as a colony in 1895, and the Japanese administration used it 18 as the means for effecting and servicing the large expansion in Taiwan's irrigated area which occurred during the colonial period (to 1945). It contrasts strikingly with the form of organisation through which all canal irrigation schemes beyond a rather small size have been built and operated in South Asia, and increasingly in Southeast Asia also: a centralised government Ministry, with headquarters in the capital city and dispersed canal offices in or near each canal command area, with staff employed by the government and (at 'professional'levels) rotated from one project to another, with operating costs coming not from beneficiaries' payments but from a regular government grant.

This latter form of organisation generates recurrent problems of motivation and information feedback. 19   There are no obvious mechanisms by which canal managers could reap some economic (or prestige) benefits by improved water allocation; nor are there likely to be other mechanisms by which canal managers can be kept directly accountable to farmers. Moreover, this form of organisation is unsuitable for generating a sense of 'moral involvement' on the part of staff with their job and organisation, which

might, even in the absence of specific material
rewards or mechanisms of accountability, lead them
to perform their job conscientiously. It also
tends to be more suited to downward flows of
directives from the top than to upward flows of
information from the field, partly just because of
the geographical distance between levels, partly
because of social class or status distance. The
effect of these features of the centralised,
departmental form of irrigation organisation is that
canal managers tend to place more weight on avoiding
the social conflict which rationing water is likely
to generate than on capturing the full economic
gains from efficient use of water.

This is a good part of the reason why planners
and funding agencies have often been dismayed that
the initial project plans bear little resemblance to
the final achievement; because their plans assume
a degree of managerial control over water which is
not reached in most projects throughout South and
Southeast Asia even where the physical structures
permit.

The Irrigation Associations of Japan and Taiwan
seem to provide a structure of incentives and
accountability which will ameliorate these problems.
Yet while much is known about the form of Irrigation
Associations (their organisational structure and
rules), [20] detailed studies of how they function in
practice are lacking.

South Korean agriculture has received little
scholarly attention compared to Japan's or Taiwan's,
and its irrigation organisation has received much
less.   Its irrigation organisation clearly belongs
to the same family; like Taiwan's it was introduced
from Japan at the start of the colonial period, in
the early years of the twentieth century.   But there
are no published studies even of the structure, rules
and operating procedures, let alone of how the form
of organisation actually works in Korean conditions;
so we simply do not know how similar or different it
is to Taiwan's. This book aims to contribute to the
comparative study of irrigation organisation by
reducing that gap.

OUTLINE

There are thus two distinct but overlapping
themes: one is state control in an authoritarian,
fast-growing state, using irrigation (and agriculture more generally) as the context; the second is
irrigation organisation itself, with the South

Korean model being studied in relation to Taiwan's, with occasional glances at India's.

Chapter 2 gives a summary picture of South Korea's agriculture, irrigation history, and public administration. Chapter 3 introduces the FLIA which we take as an example of the FLIA form of organisation. Chapter 4 describes how this FLIA organises its ostensible main functions, of water delivery, canal maintenance and agricultural extension. Chapter 5 examines relations between FLIA staff and irrigators, and between 'government' and farmers more generally. Chapter 6 considers the internal structure and operation of the FLIA, and its relations with central government. Chapter 7 discusses the proposed FLIA reform, and draws some broader conclusions about the comparative study of irrigation organisation. Chapter 8 links conclusions from the study of the FLIA to the opposing interpretations of South Korea's development to which I briefly referred earlier. Students of irrigation organisation may wish to read all the chapters except the last; students of politics may wish to skip lightly over Chapters 3 and 4.

NOTES

1. But there are problems in knowing how equal. Many statements about South Korean income distribution rely on Adelman's results (e.g. as in Adelman and Robinson 1978), whose methods have been powerfully critised by Bai Moo Ki 1978.

2. Little 1979 exemplifies the strengths and still more the weaknesses of a neoclassical interpretation. See also, as examples of a huge congratulatory literature, Adelman and Robinson 1978, Bergsman 1980, Rao 1978, Hasan 1976, Wade and Kim, and Brown 1973. Kuznets 1977 gives a useful overview of economic aspects. In the denunciatory mode, see Easey and McCormack 1977 ('South Korean society: the deepening nightmare'), Foster-Carter 1977, Kim Chang Soo 1979, Long 1977. The quotations are from Foster-Carter. For a powerful critique from within a Marxist sympathy of one of the main theoretical premises of the denunciatory writers, see Brenner 1977; and also Diaz-Alejandro 1978. In addition to the theoretical weaknesses suggested by the arguments of Brenner and Diaz-Alejandro, another problem of this school is that the standards by which South Korea is judged so appalling either are not made clear (an undefined socialist alternative), or are from North Korea (despite the extreme unreliab-

ility and paucity of data on North Korea, and the virtual impossibility of unsupervised visits), or are from already industrialised countries (see Long 1977, p. 37). A related problem is that apparently highly favourable indicators, such as trends in life expectancy, infant mortality, fertility, and adult literacy, tend simply to be ignored (as in Long 1977). The shrill and undiscriminating hostility of these writers may be understood as a response to the bland and undiscriminating congratulations of the first set. The 'anti' group, nonetheless, do illuminate important aspects of South Korea on which the first group is silent.

3. Amnesty International 1979, Kim Chang Soo 1977. On North Korea, see Amnesty International n.d. (1979).

4. For a general discussion of this type of development, see Wallerstein 1974.

5. This is not to say that the long-term objectives were defined in terms of an export-led growth strategy (in the ex ante sense). The long-term objectives are better understood in terms of the desire to perform better than North Korea and catch up with Japan (the envied and feared ex-colonial ruler). As Datta-Chaudhuri observes, 'it is fair to say that Korean policy-makers do not make any strategic differentiation between import substitution and export promotion' (1979, p. 24). See Chapter 8.

6. Financial Times 1979 and 1980, Hasan 1976, Korea Exchange Bank 1980. Compare Foster-Carter 1977, Long 1979, as illustrations of crude dependency theory, and for more general expositions see Frank 1976 and Amin 1974.

7. Datta-Chaudhuri 1979, p. 16. The calculation is based on the size of government savings (excess of taxation over current expenditure) plus deposits in the (wholly nationalised) banking system, plus foreign investment (all of which the government has to approve).

8. An important exception is Jones and SaKong 1978, to which I am indebted in my formulation of the implementation problem (their work in turn owes much to Dahl and Lindblom 1953). However, as an explanation of South Korea's development, their argument gives inadequate weight to the international context and the geo-political significance of South Korea within it. See also Datta-Chaudhuri 1979.

9. Here I follow Apthorpe's observation on Taiwan, 1979, p. 520. See relatedly Marx's Pre-

Capitalist Economic Formations, 1964, p. 33-35.

10. Marx elaborated the idea of an 'Asiatic mode of production' first in articles and letters on India (1853) and later, with less emphasis on the causal primacy of irrigation, in Pre-Capitalist Economic Formations. Wittfogel 1963 develops a rival concept of 'Oriental despotism', and (partially) summarises and cites sources for Marx's writings on the Asiatic mode of production, pp. 372-77.

11. See Hunt and Hunt 1976, Bennett 1974, Mitchell 1973, Lees 1974, Wade 1979.

12. Brandt Commission (Independent Commission on International Development Issues), 1980, p. 94.

13. Gravity-flow surface-water irrigation as distinct from pumped groundwater irrigation.

14. For example, 'The current case for improved water and soil management must be reconciled with the historical evidence of the last three decades that many investments in large-scale water and land development projects in poor nations gave a relatively low "payoff"' (Pereira et al. 1979, p. 42). See also National Research Council 1977, Vol. II, p. 71, 124, Government of India, Irrigation Commission, 1972, Wade 1980.

15. Colombo et al. 1977.

16. Bottrall 1978 for a succinct statement of some of the issues. See further Wade and Chambers 1980, Wade 1980.

17. But see my forthcoming book and a mimeographed long paper by Pant 1979, also Wade 1980, Moore 1980.

18. Presumably without elected farmers' representatives.

19. See Wade 1980, Levine 1977, Crosson 1975.

20. See for example Abel 1975 and references therein, Levine et al. 1976. Apthorpe 1979 remarks on the paucity of serious studies of Irrigation Associations in Taiwan.

2
South Korean Agriculture, Administration and Irrigation

CLIMATE AND SOILS

South Korea belongs to the category of temperate climate Asian rice producers, like the northern provinces of Japan and China in and north of the Yangtze River valley. It has a monsoon climate, intermediate between the continental climate of China and the maritime climate of Japan,[1] with clearly distinguished seasons. The winter is dry and cold, with sub-freezing temperatures, the summer is humid and hot. The country's northerly latitude brings long hours of daylight during the growing season, which is a very favourable influence on crop yields. On the other hand, the frost-free period (175 days in the north and 220 days in the south) is too short to permit more than one irrigated rice crop a year.

The average annual rainfall exceeds 1,200 mm in most places, 60 percent of it between July and September.[2] The high seasonal variability makes for a wide range in maximum and minimum flow of rivers, and heavy rainfall during the summer frequently causes flood damage to crops.

Soils are loam or silt loam in flat lowland paddy fields, and silt loams, silty clay or clay loams in upland areas. In both areas the clay content is low and the soils generally not heavy; but the high silt content causes soil drainage problems, making a winter crop of barley difficult in some areas of the southern and central parts of the country (where the climate is mild enough to permit a second grain crop).

CROPPING AND SETTLEMENT

From April to September the alluvial plains and upland valleys of South Korea are blanketed in rice. There is a concentration of settlement, intensive farming, and irrigation development for rice cultivation on the alluvial plains along the western and southern coastal areas. Rice is grown in the lowlands and terraced valleys; upland crops, orchards, and village compounds

are located on foothills bordering the paddy fields; and
wood lots and forest trees are found at higher altitudes.
Almost all the rice is irrigated, mostly from myriad
reservoirs, ponds, springs, weirs across rivers (groundwater is little used), each facility normally irrigating
less than 50 hectares.

Only a little more than two million hectares (a fifth
of the total area) is cultivated; of which 58 percent is
under rice, 42 percent under upland crops.[3] Overall,
about half the cultivated area is double cropped, more
in the south and less in the north, with (unirrigated)
barley the main second crop. With a total population of
37 million (1978) and a gross cultivated area of 3.1
million hectares (counting each double cropped hectare
twice), South Korea's population density per gross
cultivated hectare is amongst the highest in the world.
The rice area per head of national population is only
0.035 hectares.

About half of the national population is classed as
'rural' (living in settlements of less than 5,000 people).
The 2.3 million farm households (1977) are scattered into
some 35,000 tightly nucleated villages, of an average
size of 74 households, or 390 people.[4] Rapid urbanisation
over the past decade has reduced the proportion of the
national population in farm households from a half in
1966 to a third in 1978, slightly easing the pressure of
population on the land (raising the average cultivated
area per farm household from 0.90 hectares to 0.99 hectares).

LAND, LABOUR AND TECHNOLOGY

In 1937, towards the end of Korea's period as a
Japanese colony, only about a fifth of farm households
owned all the land they worked, and over half were pure
tenants, leasing in land from relatively large landowners.
The post-Independence land reform of 1948/50 established
a structure of family proprietorships, with most families
owning the land they worked. By 1965 only 7 percent
were pure tenants, and few landowners held more than
three hectares. By the standards of other 'mixed'
economies, the distribution of agricultural land ownership is still extraordinarily equal in South Korea, and
not even in the 1970s, as concentrations of private
economic wealth have built up rapidly, is there much
evidence that absentee landlordism has been on the
increase.[5]

The extraordinary homogeneity in size of holdings
gives rise to a striking uniformity of production conditions and production organisation. South Korean
villages are made up overwhelmingly of single-family
households engaged in full-time farming; most farm only
their own lands, some are part tenants, a few are pure

tenants, and even fewer are agricultural labour households.
Most farmers grow a large part of their own food requirements, and remain unintegrated into vertical food processing and manufacturing complexes. Rice is everywhere the
main crop, supplying over half of total agricultural
income; conversely, diversification into other less land-
using production with higher potential returns (such as
livestock, sericulture) has been slow. Labour is provided
from within the family; labour exchange groups are commonly formed for meeting the sharp seasonal peaks at
transplanting and harvesting, though wage labour at
these times is now more common, especially for women, as
rural labour shortages have become acute in the 1970s.[6]
About a quarter of total labour input per farm household
is non-family labour; and even the smallest class of
farm size requires non-family labour at planting and
harvesting.[7] In the 1960s and early 1970s the proportion
of total farm household income from off-farm sources
(including agricultural labour) has been about a fifth
(much less than Japan and Taiwan); but has recently
started to rise.

There is relatively little difference between farm
sizes in terms of technology, use of 'modern' inputs
like chemical fertiliser and insecticides, cropping
patterns, and yields. By South Asian standards labour
inputs per crop per hectare remain high.[8] Rural labour
shortage is the problem, not rural unemployment.

Mechanisation is now extensive in threshing and
winnowing, water lifting, plant protection (manual or
motorised chemical sprayers), ploughing and harrowing
(two-wheeled tractors); but is only now beginning for
harvesting and transplanting, the most labour-intensive
operations of all, and weeding is still done mainly by
hand. Steel-framed vinyl vegetable-growing houses are
common. Overall, the level of mechanisation is still
far below that of Japan and Taiwan, the dependence on
human and animal draught power still far greater;[9] but
compared with South Asia, the level of mechanisation is
extraordinarily high.

Chemical fertiliser use has increased rapidly since
the 1950s (at almost 9 percent per annum between 1956 and
1970),[10] to levels which are now exceptionally high by
international standards.[11] Pest control treatments are
intensely used. At the start of the 1970s new higher
yielding paddy varieties (HYVs) suitable for temperate
climates were introduced, subsequently spreading rapidly
- according to the statistics, to almost half the paddy
area by 1976.[12]

In the late 1960s a big increase in the area under
irrigation occurred, raising the 'fully irrigated' rice
area from 58 percent in 1968 to 80 percent in 1970; by
1977 the figure had been raised to 85 percent.[13]

FOOD OUTPUT AND CONSUMPTION

While the growth rates of South Korean agriculture
have been respectable by international standards, they
have not been rapid enough to keep up with food demand
(nor, unsurprisingly, with growth of industrial output).
But relatively slow rates of agricultural growth in the
1960s, during the period of rapid expansion of manufactured exports, were followed by rapid increases in the
1970s. Most of the increases came from growth of yields
rather than area, and most of the yield increases came
from rice, due particularly to the spread of the HYVs
and high levels of fertilisers. In 1961-62 paddy rice
yields averaged 309 kilograms per 0.1 hectares; in 1968-
70, 317; and by 1975, 397.[14] South Korea now claims the
highest average rice yields per hectare per crop in the
world.[15]
Rice, the basic foodstuff, accounts for over 40
percent of the food expenditure of urban households, and
over half of the (imputed) food expenditure of rural
households.[16] Rice imports were high in the second half
of the 1960s and early 1970s, but since the mid 1970s
have been small or zero. But imports of other grains
(mainly wheat and corn) have increased steadily since
the early 1970s, and now (1978) total grain imports by
weight are equal to just under half total rice production.
The growing foreign exchange cost of food imports is one
reason why the government has given more attention to
agriculture in the 1970s after the relative neglect of
the 1960s.

GOVERNMENT POLICIES

The Japanese colonial government developed Korea,
like Taiwan, as a supplier of rice for the Japanese
population. Ishikawa's description of Japanese policies
in Taiwan applies also to Korea: '...expansion in
irrigation and drainage, dissemination of improved or
better seeds, and spread in the use of fertilisers and
manures were all energetically attempted, sometimes even
with the aid of the police force' (1967, p.102). The
result was a technological level in Korean agriculture
high by standards in South and Southeast Asia; and the
colonists' interest in rice, the subsistence food crop,
prevented the emergence of the 'dualism' familiar in
agricultures which have undergone Western colonial rule,
between a plantation export agriculture and a low technology 'subsistence' food producing agriculture. However,
harsh compulsory procurement of rice prevented the
producers from deriving much benefit from the rising output.
The post-Independence governments, especially that
of President Park Chung-hee (1961-79), were actively and

pervasively interventionist in agriculture as in
industry, as had been the Japanese. The government
blocked a free market in land, thereby preventing any
marked inequality in land ownership to emerge after the
land reform (although the rapid industrialisation was
probably a more important influence on that result).[17]
The government has also monopolised the supply of chemical
fertiliser and institutional credit; and it attempts to
closely control the agencies which operate all but very
small canal irrigation systems.

Requisitioning of rice and barley was continued after
Independence, at prices always well below market levels
and sometimes below cost of production. The depressing
effect on food supply from domestic production was offset by vast inflows of US food aid and concessional sales.
The cheap food policy worsened living conditions in the
countryside (compulsory procurement constituted an important hidden tax on agriculture); but it facilitated the
export boom of the 1960s, by allowing wages in manufacturing to be kept relatively low.

After the squeeze and neglect of the 1950s and 1960s,
agriculture and rural development in the 1970s has been
enjoying much greater attention, and this for several
reasons. One is the rural unrest of the late 1960s and
early 1970s, as rural incomes fell further behind urban
incomes; one expression of which was the loss of crucial
rural support for President Park in the 1971 presidential
elections, despite government mechanisms to ensure his
success at the polls. Another is the influx of rural
migrants to the cities and towns in excess of jobs,
creating a potentially unstable marginal population on
the urban peripheries. And a third was the rapidly
rising foreign exchange cost of food imports, as US food
aid and concessional sales were cut off in the early
1970s. These factors, and especially the marginal electoral victory of President Park, gave rise to deep
governmental concern. Changes in agricultural policies,
already under way, were accelerated.

The third Five-Year Plan (1971-76) was designed to
bring rural incomes up to urban levels, and to reach
self-sufficiency in the two most important foodgrains,
rice and barley. The strategy had four main elements:
(1) The HYV programme to spread the new seeds and very
high levels of chemical and natural fertiliser. (2) A
high rice and barley price policy, by which government
agrees to buy a certain (high) proportion of farmers'
HYV rice and barley at above market prices, and in this
way to transfer income into (not out of, as in the 1950s
and 1960s) the countryside. (3) Continued heavy investment in infrastructure (roads, irrigation facilities,
paddy land rearrangement); though government investment
outlays for agriculture were planned to, and did in fact
remain a constant proportion (about one quarter) of total

government investment, as in the 1960s. (4) The <u>Saemaul</u>
(New Community) Movement, a community development programme under which villagers were brought together to
contribute labour (and in principle, directive decision-
making) for the construction of local infrastructure
(improved village access roads, drinking water supply,
stream bank lining) - and also, equally importantly, to
be educated in 'nation building' and the achievements of
the Park government, and to create an atmosphere of concerted responsiveness to the government's 'guidance'
(especially on HYV's).

In the late 1970s pressures have been building up to
abandon the second arm of the strategy - the high rice
price policy, which has raised the producer price to over
twice the world market price - in favour of greater
reliance on food imports, in order to lower the cost of
food (and permit urban wages to be kept lower than otherwise, hence exports more competitive); also to release
more labour from agriculture for more productive use, and
at the same time to reduce the inflationary effect of the
massive rice and barley subsidies (which in recent years
have ranged from $\frac{1}{2}$ to 2 percent of GNP, according to
official, probably downward biased estimates).[18] There
is also growing disquiet at the heavy dependence on
imported petroleum (South Korea produces none) which the
striving for food self-sufficiency via intensive application of chemicals has generated.

The emphasis on barley has now been much softened,
because its June harvest invades the optimal time for
rice land operations, and winter vegetables under vinyl
offer wealthier farmers much higher returns where marketing permits; but the change in barley policy came not
before the government attempted to increase barley consumption by requiring lunches carried by schoolchildren
and restaurant meals to contain a certain minimum proportion of barley to rice - an order enforced by teachers
on the one hand and special police inspection units on
the other.

RURAL LIVING LEVELS

A South Korean sociologist relates the following
incident:

>During the course of a village study in the late
>1950s I made a routine stop at a farm-house to
>conduct an interview. To my surprise the lady
>of the house was clutching a child in her arms
>who appeared to be practically dead. When asked
>why the child had not been rushed to the hospital
>she replied she had to wait for her husband. Upon
>further enquiry I learned that her husband had gone

out early that morning to raise the 500 <u>hwan</u>
needed to take the child to the hospital <u>and</u>
had not returned yet.

He continues,

In those days there were many households in Korean
farming villages as poor as this. Not a few kept
themselves alive by eating grass roots and the
bark of trees in the spring when their stock of
grains had been exhausted. Every village had a
few households which just barely kept going on
the strength of government relief. Any household which did have a small surplus sent its
children to middle school or perhaps high school.
Many of these young people failed to find employment after graduation and simply returned to the
village. The villages were full of young men in
their teens just loafing around. Their lack of
enthusiasm for farm work combined with the typical
farmer's work ethic which made this leisure
detestable was a constant source of friction. In
most villages there was no electricity. Radios
were also virtually non-existent although there
were a few houses with a homemade 'crystal radio'..
(Lee, Man-gap 1978, p.10).

There can be little doubt, even allowing for the unreliability of the statistics, that the improvement in
material living levels since the late 1950s has been
dramatic, both bigger in terms of averages and more
equally distributed than in rural areas of South and
Southeast Asia. Life expectancy, for example, is 68
years for the population as a whole (compared to Taiwan's
72, India's 51, Bangladesh's 46, Sri Lanka's 65,
Malaysia's 68, Indonesia's 48).[19] By 1972 over 90 percent of the adult population (rural and urban) was
classed as literate, nearly all children attended
primary school, over 40 percent attended secondary
school, and 33 percent of higher enrolment was in agriculture and engineering.[20] (But even in the 1950s
education enrolments were as high in South Korea as in
countries with two or three times South Korea's average
income per head.)[21] And there is one TV set for 1.5
households nationally;[22] in villages, every second or
third household commonly has one.[23] Electric rice
cookers, electric fans, transistor radios, are still
more common. In short, people can expect to have a
much longer illness-free life than in the 1950s or
before, or than is now normal in South or Southeast
Asia, and to be able through education and consumer
goods to enjoy that life.

On the other side, rural people are allowed little influence on or even unrestrained discussion of issues of
government policy which affect them deeply, and are
subject to considerable coercion at the hands of local
officials (Chapter 5). They are subject also to a
stream of propaganda invoking constant vigilance against
invasion and internal subversion, and young men are
required to do three years' compulsory military service.
It must also be said that the dramatic increases in
farm housholds' real income has taken place mostly since
the early 1970s (when the high rice price policy was
introduced); indeed real incomes may even have fallen
during the 1960s. And while the government's claim that
the gap in average income per household between rural
and urban areas has been narrowing since the late 1960s
is probably correct, the claim that by 1974 average
rural incomes had surpassed average urban incomes seems
quite implausible.[24] Nevertheless, however recent the
improvements, however severe the compulsion through
which many were effected, however much many 'improvements' represent cosmetic changes for travellers along
national highways, however limited the rights of political expression and civil liberties, what is difficult
to deny is that the rural population in South Korea has
experienced a much larger increase in material living
standards, including the standards which really matter
for welfare, than the rural population of virtually any
country of South or Southeast Asia.[25] The farmers I
talked with revelled in their new-found comforts, and I
entirely sympathise.

Yet it is not true that farmers on the whole are
content with their life as farmers and countrydwellers.
A recent survey of over 500 farmers in different parts
of the country found that only a quarter said they
wanted their children to remain on the land.[26] Most
farmers aspire to live in the city (especially Seoul),
and if they can't make it themselves they are trying to
put their children in a position to do so, particularly
by heavy investment in their education. In the same
survey 70 percent of the farmers said they would like to
send their children to college (after high school), and
for most respondents, children's education was said to
have first claim on extra income from farming. Educational qualification is a ladder out of the countryside.
In short, the agricultural prosperity which has come in
the past decade is being used to provide the means for
moving out of agriculture and the countryside.

ADMINISTRATIVE STRUCTURE

The South Korean polity and political culture emphasises
authority, hierarchy, bureaucratic order, and experience
of popular representation is almost wholly lacking.

Before the end of the nineteenth century, Korea was a self-governing, centralised, bureaucratic-agrarian kingdom, modelled closely in its political and administrative institutions on China, whence came much of its higher culture - ritual, script, ethics, fine arts, and Buddhism.[27] Representative political institutions based on universal suffrage were introduced after Independence in 1945, at national and local levels. The 1961 military government abolished local elective councils and made the government responsible for appointing previously elected local officials (such as the village chief and the township chief); but otherwise made few changes in local administrative structure. For most of the post-1945 period a National Assembly has existed, composed in part of elected representatives, but has been permitted only marginal influence in governance. The executive branch has overwhelmingly dominated both the legislature and the judiciary.

Post-Independence rulers (like their predecessors) have tended to take a bleak view of the populace at large, seeing their unconstrained political impluses as the source of chaos and instability and lack of economic growth. Even during the 1945-61 period, and still more since 1961, they have emphasised the need for control from above. This control has come not via a mass political party - no party has anything like a mass membership - but through the governmental bureaucracy itself.

The country is divided into 9 provinces, 33 cities, 138 counties (gun). Each county has a county town (eup), generally of 20-50,000 people, and sub-counties or townships (myon), each with a government administrative office. The second to lowest administrative unit is the ri, either a single village or several hamlets. The ri is divided into ban, groupings of 14-20 neighbouring households. In 1975 each ri had an average of 74 households, or 389 poeple. There was an average of 27 ri in each township or subcounty (myon), and 10 myon to each county. Except in the mountains, most villages are within 10 kilometres of a township office. This office is staffed by full-time government officials, mostly local people. By South Asian standards this density of government administrative offices and personnel is very high.

The network of government ministries and agencies which influence agricultural development and rural living is dominated by the Ministry of Home Affairs, the most important ministry in the apparatus of rural social control. It combines the dual responsibilities of coercive control via the police with administrative control over all other government agencies at provincial and local levels. It appoints the county chief and the

township chief; and the provincial governors are directly
responsible to and supervised by it.

The county chief coordinates and supervises all
government units within the county. The county, more
than the province or the township, is the executive unit
in rural development. However, it has little room for
autonomous decisions; 80 percent of county funds are
provided from the centre, and major initiatives come
from Seoul.[28]

While the Ministry of Home Affairs' authority over
local government units gives it considerable de facto
influence over agricultural production and marketing
programmes, substantive responsibility for the latter is
with the Ministry of Agriculture and Fisheries (hence-
forth, MAF). MAF is guided, in turn, by the Office of
the Prime Minister and the Economic Planning Board (which
coordinates the formulation and implementation of all
economic development plans). Within the MAF headquarters
in Seoul, separate bureaus have authority for planning
and budgeting, statistics, land and water resource
development, food grain and other price support and
purchase programmes, fertiliser distribution, credit,
marketing and production expansion programmes for crops,
livestock, sericulture and fisheries; and, notably for
our purposes, for supervision of the Farmland Improvement Associations, which operate canal irrigation systems.
These bureaus have counterpart offices in the Economic
Planning Board and in the Ministry of Home Affairs responsible for monitoring their activities. (An elaborate
structure of parallel offices and cross-monitoring
between administrative hierarchies within the bureaucracy is characteristic of South Korean public administration; it provides a means of control over any one
arm which might come from elected representatives in
more democratic polities or from a parallel structure
within the mass party in more totalitarian ones.)

While the Ministry of Agriculture has responsibility
for planning and supervising agricultural programmes,
implementation is by parastatal agencies which include
the Office for Rural Development (ORD), with responsibility for agricultural research and extension; the
National Agricultural Cooperative Federation (NACF), the
sole supplier of fertiliser and most agricultural
chemicals, the sole source of institutional agricultural
credit, and the sole agent for government grain purchases;
and the Agricultural Development Corporation (ADC), which
designs and constructs large-scale irrigation and drainage projects (with service areas of greater than 50
hectares). These parastatals can engage in business
activities and (in law) have other sources of finance
besides the government.

The ORD and the NACF are organised into provincial units, each unit directly supervised by the provincial governor and each having considerable autonomy. While the ORD and NACF organisations are thus not as far-flung from the central government control hierarchy as the FLIAs are, one can presume that our conclusions from the study of the FLIAs will also be relevant to ORD and NACF relations with central government and with their clients.

From the point of view of farmers, they have four organisations on which they depend and by which they are to some degree controlled, in addition to the county administration and its township arms: the ORD, the NACF, the Saemaul Movement, and the FLIA (for systems of over 50 hectares). Though our focus is on the latter, the other three also appear in the discussion from time to time.

IRRIGATION

Although Japan formally annexed Korea in 1910, it attained de facto political and economic control some years earlier. Amongst the first steps it took to make use of its colony was improvement of irrigation facilities. Irrigation was much better developed in Japan than in Korea; well before the middle of the nineteenth century the main outline of Japan's present-day irrigation networks had already been laid, and use of relatively sophisticated storage and control structures was common wherever rice could be grown.[29] The Japanese set out to create a similar institutional framework for irrigation as already existed in Japan. In 1906 the 'Regulations for Irrigation Work in Korea' were announced, giving the framework for state promotion of irrigation expansion; and in 1908 the first Irrigation Association was formed.[30] Up to 1920 however the main emphasis was on rehabilitation of irrigation facilities which had fallen into disrepair during the later years of the pre-Japanese dynasty. But as Japan's own deficit of rice production in relation to consumption grew, the interest in Korea and Taiwan as rice exporters to Japan also grew. In 1920 a 15 year plan to increase rice production in Korea was initiated, with two main components: expanded irrigation and land development; and adoption of improved seeds and tools through energetic (and coercive) extension. The irrigation and land development component was implemented via national parastatal agencies of the Japanese government and via Irrigation Associations, with huge government expenditure through subsidies and low-interest loans or direct investment. The irrigation works constructed under these arrangements were said to be often technologically superior to those in Japan.[31] The pace of the programme was directly related to the demand for imported rice in Japan. In 1933 a rice surplus in Japan led to the abrupt discontinuation of the programme in Korea, by which time 196 Irrigation Associations had been formed, covering an irrigated area of over 220,000 hectares, of which about 165,000 hectares were the result of the programme begun in 1920.[32] The improved supply of water made possible by these improvements in turn facilitated the dissemination of imported varieties of rice and the spread in fertiliser use. Between 1920 and 1940 average (cleaned) rice yields per hectare increased from 1.7 tons to 2.5 tons.[33] Investment in irrigation and land development again picked up in the late 1930s as war preparations in Japan increased its food deficit.

After the Second World War and then the Korean War (1950-53), land and water development projects continued to receive the largest share of government allocations to agriculture. The three five-year development plans, from 1961 to 1976, have allocated about a quarter of allocations to agriculture for irrigation and land development. The planted rice area classed as 'fully irrigated' increased from 534,000 hectares in 1955 (45 percent of the total rice area), to 729,000 hectares in 1966 (57 percent). Beginning in 1964 paddy consolidation projects assumed increasing importance in the land and water budget. They involve consolidation of small, irregularly shaped plots into larger, rectangular units, improvement of field channels and drainage ditches, installation of on-farm water control structures, and the construction of feeder roads to give better field access. At the same time, enormously expensive tideland reclamation projects came to take up much of the total budget. By 1971 over one million hectares (81 percent of the total rice area) was claimed to be fully irrigated; by 1977, 85 percent.

On the basis of evidence from both Taiwan and South Korea, Ishikawa observes[34] that the rise in their rice yields from the level reached by 1900 (the level of South and Southeast Asian countries in the 1950s and 1960s) to the level reached by 1940 (the level of Japan in the late nineteenth century) was accompanied by, first, a mild improvement of existing irrigation facilities, and then (in Korea after 1920) by a drastic expansion of technologically superior works. Irrigation played the leading input, permitting the introduction of improved varieties, increased fertiliser and other improved techniques to take place. In Japan a similar pattern is observed. Generalising, Ishikawa suggests that the fundamental requirements of productivity increase in Asian rice agriculture are, '...first, control of water and then, technological innovation, centering around the

introduction of higher-yielding varieties with high
fertiliser-response. These two continue to play the
role of leading input alternatively' (1967, pp.108-9).

However, while the pattern of productivity increase
in Taiwan, Japan and Korea has been similar, their
climatic differences make an important difference to
the significance of irrigation. In Taiwan, two or more
irrigated crops a year are climatically possible; but
the second irrigated crop is entirely dependent on
irrigation, which gives a powerful incentive to store
water and use it effectively even in the rainy season,
and therefore to devise and enforce institutional mechanisms for bringing this about. In Japan a second
irrigated crop is possible only in the southern-most
provinces; but because rainfall is relatively evenly
distributed over the year, compared to Korea, and inadequate during the growing season months, the spread
of paddy cultivation required the creation of facilities
to store and distribute rainfall and to control and
direct the flow of rivers. In Korea on the other hand,
only one irrigated crop a year is climatically possible,
as in most of Japan; but with much greater concentration
of rainfall in the growing season months than in Japan,
the amount of water that must be added by irrigation is
relatively low.

If the crop water requirement for rice is taken to
be approximated by its potential evapotranspiration, an
index of irrigation requirement can be derived by com-
paring rainfall against evapotranspiration. (The difference between evapotranspiration and rainfall, however,
does not accurately measure the volume needed to be
supplied by irrigation, because that volume has to be
greater than the amount needed by the crop to allow for
seepage, evaporation and management 'waste'.) In these
terms (using Thornthwaite's calculations)[35] the contrast
in irrigation requirement between South Korea and Taiwan
is indeed striking. In the westerly plains of Taiwan,
where most of the irrigation is concentrated, average
monthly rainfall falls short of average crop water
requirement in every month of the year except March,
which in places shows a small surplus, and in June,
July and August, which show very large surpluses of
rainfall over need. Taiwan has two main cropping
seasons, in both of which rice is the dominant crop: a
'dry' season from December to June, and a 'wet' season
from June to October; in southerly parts of the island
a brief third cropping season is available between
October and December. To make use of the long annual
growing period which temperatures make possible it is
essential that as much as possible of the surplus of
rainwater over need in June to August is stored, and
that this water plus the residual flows in the rivers

is used carefully to cover as large an area as possible
with enough irrigation to meet crop water requirements
over the rest of the year. In contrast, in the main
irrigated areas of South Korea temperatures rule out
more than one irrigated crop a year, and during the
growing season, except in places in May, there is an
average monthly surplus of rainfall over crop need; and
the May deficit, which is in any case small, can be
covered not only by irrigation but also by moisture
retained in the soil after the winter. The surpluses
are especially large during the later, grain-filling
stage of crop growth - at which time water stress if it
occurred would cause large loss of yield.

Why then is there irrigation in South Korea? The
first reason is that there are fluctuations around the
long-term average figures, and in some years these are
severe enough to cause bad droughts. In the period
between 1965 and 1979, drought hit much of the penin-
sular in 1967 and 1968, affecting a fifth to a quarter
of South Korea's paddy land and causing estimated losses
of production of 12 and 17 percent of total production,
respectively; in the other years, however, the estimated
paddy drought loss only twice amounted to more than half
of one percent (and in no case more than one percent).[36]

The second reason is that irrigation encourages the
use of much higher levels of fertiliser than would be
feasible without it. One study of 15 new small-scale
irrigation projects started in 1972 concluded that after
irrigation paddy yields increased by 50-75 percent over
rainfed paddy, holding seed variety constant; presumably
much of the increase reflected higher fertiliser use.[37]
The Japanese colonial government invested in irrigation
in Korea for just this reason. A Japanese study of
Korean agriculture in 1935 remarked:

> The first technical condition of rice production is
> nothing but water control. But paddy field in Korea
> is so-called 'rain-fed paddy field',...accordingly
> marshy paddy field with drainage difficulty, which
> is considered of low quality in Japan is considered
> good paddy field... Who would dare to apply ferti-
> lisers under such conditions? (Tobata and Ohkawa,
> quoted in Hayami and Ruttan, 1971, p.209).

On the other hand, it is also true that the Japanese
invested much less in Korean irrigation than in Taiwanese (by 1930 the proportion of paddy area which was
irrigated stood at 0.59 in Korea compared to 0.88 in
Taiwan, while Taiwan's had stood at 0.56 in 1915);[38]
it seems likely that this difference reflects not only
the decade longer involvement of Japan in Taiwan than
in Korea, and other factors suggested by Hayami and

Ruttan,[39] but also the much greater economic value of
irrigation in Taiwan.

In short, you can slop irrigation water around in
South Korea at much less economic loss than you would
incur if you ran irrigation systems in Taiwan in the
same way.

That the incentives for efficient water use in South
Korea are substantially less than in Taiwan or Japan may
help to explain why the maintenance of irrigation facilities is said to be poor (though what constitutes 'poor'
and 'good' is not indicated, and there is little evidence
from Japan or Taiwan on which a comparative judgement
could be based; though one's impression from accounts
of irrigation in those countries suggests that maintenance is considerably better).[40] For South Korea, Oh Ho-
Sung, reporting the results of a survey of some 64 small
reservoirs (with a command area of less than 50 hectares),
says that, 'The general maintenance condition of the
small reservoirs was so poor that approximately 64 percent of the sample reservoirs would not have a depend-
able water supply in case of a drought which may occur
in ten years' (1978, p.97).[41]

Pal-Yong Moon, commenting on facilities with command
areas of more than 50 hectares, says that while it is
difficult to know with any accuracy, 'the facilities
installed after World War II are believed to be well
done, but are considerably obsolescent due to lack of
repair in scores of years, impeding their function of
irrigation and drainage. There are many facilities
requiring replacement or completely new work' (1978,
p.39). Moon also mentions in passing that 'political
intervention in the selection of projects, coupled with
lack of technology on the part of the undertakers,
caused many of the irrigation projects [especially those
of the 1950s] to be poorer in quality than those constructed during the period of World War II' (1974, p.40).

A World Bank report states that irrigation, drainage
and flood control structures are less highly developed
in South Korea than in Japan and Taiwan; and continues,
'Water control facilities are not well developed and
there are potentials for increasing crop production by
making more effective use of water resources' (World
Bank 1973, Annex 6, p.6). The report suggests that
there has been over-investment in land consolidation at
the expense of improvements in water supply, and over-
emphasis on farm drainage ditches to the neglect of
area-wide drainage systems.

To evaluate these criticisms thoroughly one would
need to know more about actual crop losses due to water
stress over a period of ten years or more, and about the
implicit criteria of good and bad maintenance, drainage,
and flood control. I take the evidence summarised
earlier to be sufficient for us to go forward with the

following propositions: (1) Rice crop losses due to
water stress (or flooding) in South Korea are on
average small; (2) to meet the average irrigation
requirement is not organisationally difficult; (3)the
reported poor state of maintenance may be due in part
to the lack of incentive for better maintenance since
even with poorly maintained structures the average
irrigation requirement can be met without difficulty;
(4) one would not expect the organisations in charge
of running canals to be much concerned about, or expert
in, making efficient use of water. This fourth proposition is a principal theme of the later discussion.

IRRIGATION ORGANISATION

Most irrigation in South Korea takes place from springs,
small reservoirs, ponds, weirs, and other facilities
which irrigate less than 50 hectares each.   There
are over 18,000 reservoir irrigation systems, of which
15,000 irrigate less than 50 hectares. However the
distinction between gravity-flow and pump-fed systems
is not sharp in South Korea (in contrast to South Asia):
many reservoir systems also use pumps, to lift river
water to the reservoir, to lift canal water to higher
ground, to re-use drainage water.   Irrigation operations
are thus typically dependent on electricity or
diesel-powered pumps - so irrigation, like cultivation,
is heavily dependent on imported petroleum. [42]
     The distinction between facilities which irrigate
more and less than 50 hectares is important
organisationally. Those with more than 50 hectares are
planned and constructed by the Ministry of Agriculture
through the Agricultural Development Corporation (ADC).
After completion they are handed over to Farmland
Improvement Associations (FLIAs), parastatal agencies
supervised by the Ministry of Agriculture, for operation
and maintenance. Smaller systems are planned and
constructed by city and county authorities, and then[43]
handed over to autonomous organisations of farmers.
The latter have to pay no part of constructions costs. [44]
     Since this essay is about the operation of FLIAs,
one needs to remember that most irrigation in South
Korea takes place outside the jurisdiction of a FLIA:
in 1977, of the 1,104,000 hectares of 'fully irrigated'
land, only 401,600 hectares (36 percent) were under a
FLIA, the rest in smaller, scattered systems.   However,
the distinction between less than and more than 50
hectare facilities is now becoming blurred, as the
government is attempting to bring all (surface-flow)
facilities within the jurisdiction of a single FLIA per

county. (So the FLIA we shall study has a few reservoirs within its jurisdiction of less than 50 hectares command area.)

Today's FLIAs are the direct descendants of the Irrigation Associations created by the Japanese (with an intermediate change of name in the 1960s to Land Development Associations). It is not clear how much, if any, change in function occurred with the change from Japanese to Korean rule. In any case, it is clear that the three main official functions of both the Irrigation Associations of the Japanese period and the FLIAs are (1) irrigation systems operation, (2) system maintenance, and (3) land development for irrigation. The FLIAs collect water charges from the beneficiaries, and use this revenue to hire engineers, agriculturalists, accountants, workmen, to carry out the functions; the charges also have to cover a portion of construction costs and land development costs. Farmers served from a less than 50 hectares system within a county which already has a FLIA are being encouraged to join it, though legally at least, the written approval of at least two thirds of the beneficiaries is needed before this can happen. The government wishes to reduce the total number of FLIAs to only one per county in the interests of saving administrative costs, making each remaining one larger in order to spread overheads. The number of FLIAs has thus fallen in the past decade from 269 in 1968 to 122 in 1978, and the average planted area per FLIA has increased from 1,100 hectares to 3,100 hectares. Only twenty FLIAs in South Korea have a benefited area of over 5,000 hectares, of which three are over 20,000 hectares.

NOTES

1. Brandt and Lee 1977.
2. World Bank 1973, Vol.2. This and Vol. 3 of the same report are the main sources on climate and soils. Rainfall measurements from twelve stations in South Korea between 1970 and 1977 show that on average, total annual rainfall fell below 1,200 mm in four of the eight years, and below 1,000 mm in two (Korea, Bureau of Statistics 1979, 12, p.3).
3. MAF, 1978, Yearbook of Agricultural and Forestry Statistics 1977.
4. Brandt and Lee 1977.
5. Lee 1979, p.509, n.41. However, because the leasing of farmland is legally prohibited, information on the extent of leasing is unreliable.
6. Reed 1979.
7. MAF, 1978a, Report on the Results of Farm Household Economy Survey, pp.84-5.

8. MAF, 1978a, <u>Farm Household Economy Survey,</u> Tab. 11-1, p.84, gives man-days per ha. per year (all crops) as 185 in 1977, down from 275 in 1965. See also Ishikawa 1978.

9. Lee 1979, n.8.

10. Lee 1979, p.497

11. In 1977 average fertiliser use per ha. of agricultural land was 325 kgs.; in Japan, 387 kgs., India, 24 kgs., and the all-Asia average was 21 kgs. (FAO 1978, <u>Fertiliser Yearbook 1978</u>).

12. Lee 1979, p.497. But for reasons suggested in Chapter 4 the figures are likely to exaggerate.

13. MAF, Agricultural Development Corporation 1978, Tab. 3. Neither from this table nor from other sources consulted (including hydrologists in the Agricultural Development Corporation), is it clear what the difference between 'fully irrigated' and 'partially irrigated' paddy is, although without knowing this the significance of the 85 percent figure is unclear.

14. MAF, 1977, <u>Yearbook of Agricultural and Forestry Statistics</u>, Tab. 29.

15. According to the FAO's <u>Monthly Bulletin of Statistics</u>, January 1980, this claim is correct, for the countries included.

16. MAF, 1977, <u>Statistical Yearbook.</u>

17. Lee 1979.

18. Richardson 1979. The South Korean government supported the price at about US$762 in 1979 against a 1974-79 average world price of about $360 per metric ton.

19. Asian Development Bank 1979, Tab. 2. The figures are for years between 1972 and 1977.

20. World Bank, 1973, Vol. I. But Asian Development Bank, 1979, Tab. 2 gives 80 percent as secondary enrolment in 1972.

21. Cole and Lyman 1971, Chp. 7, n.2.

22. <u>Korea Annual 1979</u>, p.234.

23. Of the 211 rural households in 2 townships studied by Reed (1979, p.144), 60 percent owned TV sets in 1976.

24. Lee 1979, p.497, Reed 1979, p.60.

25. This remark is based not only on statistical indicators, but on personal observation in several parts of South Korea (including areas far from national highways or cities), in several states of India, and the Central Plains of Thailand, coupled with evidence on living standards in South Korea of the 1950s and before, from village studies such as Brandt 1971 and Pak Ki-Hyuk and Gamble 1975. The observation should not be taken to imply agreement with the view that South Korea somehow provides a model for other underdeveloped non-socialist states to follow.

26. Dong-il Kim 1980, E-5.

27. Brandt and Lee 1977, on which I have drawn for much of this and the following paragraph.

28. Steinberg 1980, G-2.

29. Sawada 1972, pp.124-5. I am grateful to Penny Franks for this reference.

30. Pak Ki Sung, n.d., p.29.

31. Ishikawa 1967, p.105, quoting two Japanese writers. But compare a Korean source, Pak Ki Sung, n.d., referring to facilities constructed between 1920-1933, 'But in those years , natural damages were severe... Much of the facilities were destroyed by them, so that many associations could not run well, and accordingly they could not pay back the bank loan. The government was forced to make adjustments, closing five associations, subsidising thirty-five for the reimbursement of the bank loan' (p.33).

32. Ishikawa 1967, p.105, n.62, and Pak Ki Sung n.d., p.33.

33. Ishikawa 1967, Chart 2-5.

34. Ishikawa 1967, p.108.

35. C.W. Thornthwaite Associates 1963. Total average annual rainfall in the irrigation-intensive westerly plains of both countries is roughly 1½-2 times greater in Taiwan (around 2,000 mm) than in South Korea (around 1,200 mm). The hydrologists of the Agricultural Development Corporation use the following rules of thumb for irrigation planning. Rice in Korean conditions requires a total of 1.2 metres of water over the growing season. In an average year rainfall from April to September amounts to over 1.0 metres, leaving only 0.2 metres to be supplied by irrigation, and in the worst drought likely in 10 years (a rather stringent criterion) the irrigation requirement rises to 0.7 metres or so. Of course, these figures should be broken down into sub-periods, and rainfall run-off should be allowed for. Crude though they are, they do support the argument in the text. It proved (surprisingly) difficult to get any better hydrological or agronomic data of this type in South Korea, even from the ADC. I am grateful to Gilbert Levine and Ian Carruthers for help in interpreting Thornthwaite's figures.

36. MAF statistics collated for the author by Dr. Joung-Woung Lee. There must be some doubt about the reliability of the figures (see Chapters 5 and 6), but it is not clear which way they are likely to be biased.

37. Steinberg et al. 1980, p. 4,5; Steinberg 1980a, H-2. Steinberg also gives results from a World Bank-supported irrigation project: milled rice per ha. before the project was 2.4 and 3.2 tons, for older varieties and HYVs respectively, and 4.2 and 5.0 tons post-project. But as in the study of the fifteen small projects, fertiliser level is not controlled for; and it is not wholly clear how much irrigation, if any, already

existed in the project areas, though one infers it was of little significance.

38. Hayami and Ruttan 1971, p.208.

39. Hayami and Ruttan 1971, pp.209-10.

40. See for example Eyre 1955, Vandermeer 1968, Pasternak 1968.

41. Though one should note that a once in ten year frequency of reoccurrence of drought is a relatively stringent test of a reservoir's capacity, particularly of a small reservoir (Gilbert Levine, personal communication).

42. Nearly three quarters of South Korea's electricity is generated in oil-thermal plants; the oil is imported.

43. The autonomy of these organisations seems to be wide-ranging, perhaps surprisingly in view of the 'hard state' image. See Oh 1978.

44. Oh 1978, p.97. However in contrast, officials of MAF say that irrigators under non-FLIA surface sources have to pay 30 percent of construction costs.

3
Sy Farmland
Improvement Association

The irrigation system managed by the SY FLIA[1] is in the northern part of South Korea, a few hours by car or bus from the capital. Its total irrigated area is just over 11,000 hectares, making it amongst the largest five percent of FLIAs in terms of area.

This chapter briefly describes the area, the irrigation facilities, the structure of the organisation, and its budget. The following chapter considers the principle functions performed by the FLIA: the operation of the water delivery (and drainage) system, maintenance of the same, and agricultural extension.

THE AREA AND THE IRRIGATION SYSTEM

SY FLIA has four main reservoirs, each of which irrigates more than 2,000 hectares; and another thirteen small reservoirs, only one of which commands more than 500 hectares, and the smallest, only 13 hectares (Map 3.1). (Four of the small reservoirs can feed into the main canals which run from the four big reservoirs; the rest are completely independent .) There are also twenty pump stations to lift water short distances from rivers, drainage channels or canals. And there are 153 publicly-owned tubewells in the area (of which the FLIA administers only 26, the rest being the responsibility of the county administration); they are used only in periods of water shortage. There are also many private tubewells in the area, also used only in emergencies. (Groundwater is said to be of poor quality and to depress paddy yield by its low temperature.)[2]

Three of the four main reservoirs and their canal networks were built between 1961 and 1965; the fourth in 1972. Of the thirteen small reservoirs, the oldest was built in 1942; most of the rest are from the 1950s or 60s. Hence all the systems are by 1979 old enough to have settled down into a physical and administrative 'equilibrium'; the canal staff do not have to be

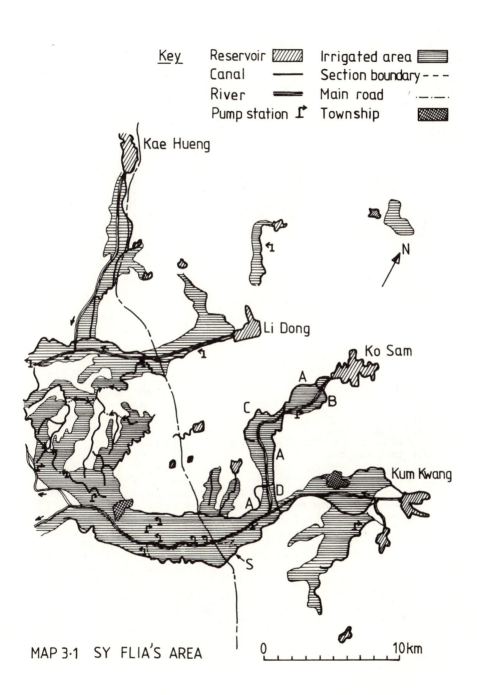

Key

Reservoir

Canal

River

Pump station

Irrigated area

Section boundary - - -

Main road

Township

Kae Hueng

N

Li Dong

Ko Sam

A

B

C

A

Kum Kwang

D

A

S

MAP 3·1 SY FLIA'S AREA

0   10km

preoccupied with sorting out the teething problems which
arise on any new irrigation scheme.   Furthermore, many,
if not a majority of farmers of the area were already
familiar with irrigation before any of the reservoirs were
built.   Paddy was then, as now, the main crop; but the
irrigation came from diversion structures on small
streams and rivers, and from groundwater.

Included in the command area are 16,750 irrigated
farms (or ownership units), covering 11,220 irrigated
hectares.   Fifty percent of the farms are less than 0.5
irrigated hectares, and account for 23 percent of the
irrigated area.   Another 29 percent are between 0.5 and
1.0 hectares, and account for another 29 percent of the
area.   Farms of over one irrigated hectare account for
only 21 percent of the number, and 48 percent of the area,
of which those over three hectares account for less than
one percent of the number and 5 percent of the area.
Total farm sizes would be greater than these figures
suggest, because the figures include only irrigated area;
but the non-irrigated cultivated area is smaller than
the paddy area. [3]   Because the area is relatively close
to Seoul and contains three sizable towns (of 60-80,000
people), it is likely that farm households in this area
receive more than the national average of 28 percent
(1978) of their income from non-agricultural sources.
Nevertheless the above figures on household/land ratios
show that population pressure on the paddy land is very
high: if we assume (as is a reasonable approximation)
that each ownership unit corresponds to a household and
that each household has five persons, there is an average
of about 0.1 hectares of paddy land per farm household
member.   Tenancy exists on a very limited scale, most
of the cultivated land being owned by the operator. [4]

Paddy is virtually the only irrigated crop, and
there is only one paddy crop a year.   19 percent of the
paddy area is cropped during the winter, mostly with
vegetables, and this is the only land which is cropped
more than once a year.   The cropping intensity of 119
is higher than the provincial average of only 107. [5]

Rice yields in the SY area are about the same as
the national average of 5 tons per hectare (1977), and
higher than the provincial average of 4.8 tons per
hectare in the same year.   Chemical fertiliser
application runs at 450 to 750 kilograms per hectare;
plus an estimated 6 to 8 tons of non-chemical fertilisers [6]

Mechanisation, here as elsewhere in South Korea, has
intensified rapidly in the past few years.   Water is now
lifted almost always by mechanical pump.   By 1977 there
was on average one power thresher to 10 planted hectares
and 14 farm households; and for both power sprayers
(used in plant protection) and two-wheeled tractors, one

per 7.5 planted hectares, and 11 farm households.[7]
The 1979 ratio of two-wheeled tractors to farm households
is estimated to be about one tractor to 8 households.
On the other hand, it is estimated that 40 percent of
the paddy area is still prepared by animal ploughing. [8]
And there has been little mechanisation as yet of
transplanting and harvesting, though this stage is
now being embarked upon with Ministry of Agriculture
and FLIA promotion.

Despite the intense pressure of population on the
land, this is not a poor area. In terms of consumer
durables, for example, all rural households have
electricity, most have piped water supply, electric fans,
electric rice cookers; many have refrigerators, tele-
visions, large portable radio/cassette players, a few
have washing machines and in each village several
households (out of normally less than eighty) have a
telephone. Very few farm households own cars, however.
Roads from main road to village tend to have poor,
unsealed surfaces which cut up badly in the heavy summer
rains and the winter snow. The public spaces in the
villages are bare earth. Food preparation (apart from
rice) is still almost wholly unmechanised, and absorbs
a great deal of women's time.

By South and Southeast Asian comparison what is
remarkable about these villages (and the same is true
elsewhere in Korea) [9] is not only the high average
material level of living, but also the equality of
living conditions between households and the absence of
material deprivation and insecurity of a degree which is
common throughout South and Southeast Asia. The range
in levels of housing, clothing, shoes, consumer goods
(the most obvious indicators to the rural visitor) is
small. This is due not only to the land reform of the
1940s and 1950s, but also to industrial growth in the
second half of the 1960s and the early 1970s which has
helped to keep villages relatively homogeneous, as the
poorer and the wealthier have left for the cities.

SY FLIA'S ORGANISATION

For its irrigated area of 11,200 hectares, SY FLIA
has a total staff of 286.(In addition to the 11,200
hectares another 2,200 hectares are newly developed and
brought under (pump) command but not yet irrigated as
of the 1979 season.) The main organisational units are
shown in Figure 3.1. The headquarter staff is divided
into three bureaus, each of which is divided into
sections. The sections of the Administration bureau
are self-explanatory. It is interesting to note how
responsibilities within the Management bureau are
divided: a section responsible for

FIGURE 3.1

Organisation Chart of SY FLIA

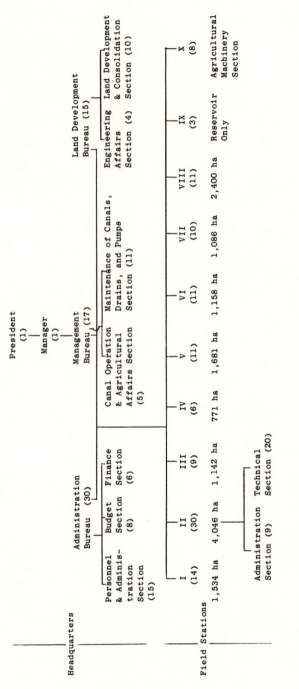

Notes: (8) - number of staff (excluding patrollers)
1,142 ha - irrigable area

canal (and pump station) <u>operation</u> as well as for
'agricultural affairs' (agricultural extension), and a
second section responsible for <u>maintenance</u> of all
irrigation and drainage facilities. This contrasts with
the more common method of organisation in large-scale
irrigation systems elsewhere in the Third World, where the
same unit (and person) handles both operation and
maintenance responsibilities within its specific area, and
the organisation for agricultural extension is quite
separate. It would seem that the South Korean division
of responsibility is the more sensible, since the skills
and orientation required for canal operation are quite
different from those needed for canal maintenance, and
closer to those needed for agricultural extension. The
third bureau, of Land Development, is responsible for the
programme of levelling, consolidating, rectangularising
paddy holdings, and fieldchannel and drainage channel
construction, which has been going on since 1965;
8,600 hectares have now been improved in this way.
Sixty-four of the staff work in the headquarters (HQ)
building, in one or other of the three bureaus and
seven sections. Another ninety-three work in the ten
Field Stations. Eight of the ten Field Stations are
concerned with the daily operation and maintenance of the
canals and pumps, and with agricultural guidance. (One
of the other two is a new section to look after the FLIA's
agricultural and canal maintenance machinery, including
a few front-end earth movers and four-wheeled tractors
for use in land development and canal maintenance, as
well as power sprayers and other light implements for
hiring to farmers and, as of 1979, its thirteen
mechanical rice transplanters. The section also
maintains the FLIA's three jeeps and one pick-up truck.)
    The Field Station staff are divided into two
sections: Administration, and Technical Affairs. The
organisation chart for one such office is shown in Figure
3.2. Note that the distinction between the maintenance
function, and the operational function combined with
agricultural guidance, is followed at this as well as
at HQ level.
    Attached to each Field office but working dispersed
throughout the command area are pump station attenders
and canal patrollers. Each of the twenty pump stations
has a full-time attender, who lives adjacent to the
station. The patrollers look after an average of about
100 hectares of irrigated land each, in a few cases as
much as 150 hectares. Their job is to patrol the main
and branch canals in their area twice a day (by bicycle).
They adjust the level of the gates and check that
the structures are in good repair. Once a day they
read the gauge levels and communicate the results
to their Field Office. Much of the small maintenance
work is carried out by each patroller himself,

FIGURE 3.2

Organisation of a Field Station Office (Section I, irrigated
area about 1,500 hectares)

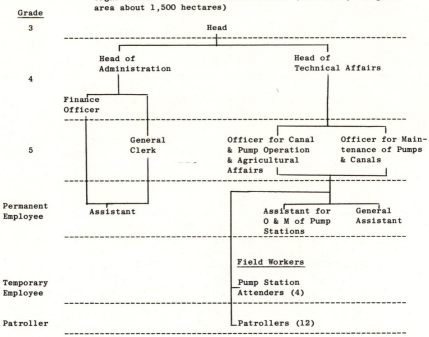

perhaps with the assistance of a patroller from an adjacent
beat. They also liaise with the pump station operator
(if any), and tell him when more or less water is needed.
And they are meant to help spot pest and disease attacks,
and give advice to farmers about what to do by way of
counter-measures.

The staff are divided into four main categories:
(1) professional staff, graded from 1 (highest) to 5,
for whom promotion between grades is possible and
expected; (2) permanent employees, who do semi-skilled
technical work or clerical work; (3) temporary employees,
who do the same range of activities as permanent
employees but on a yearly contract and paid on a daily
wage scale (they include the pump station attenders);
(4) patrollers, who are employed for six months a year
during the irrigation season, also on a daily wage basis.
The professional staff account for 35 percent of the total;
permanent and temporary employees for another 27 percent;
patrollers for 38 percent   (Tables 3.1 & 3.2).

A large majority of the staff are local people, born
and brought up in the command area or close to it. This
includes not only the patrollers (who must be resident
in the particular area they patrol) and employees, but
also the professional staff; though while the patrollers
are villagers and farmers, most of the professional staff
are from town-based, non-farming families, and virtually
none now live in villages.   There is no minimum formal
educational qualification to join as a professional
staffer (nor as employee or patroller).   Entry to grade
5 is by competitive examination or by promotion from the
ranks of permanent employees.   Increasingly entry is
being gained by the examination route, and with that
comes a lowering of the average age of grade 5 staff and
an increase in their formal educational qualifications.
Further details on recruitment are left till later.
At this point it needs to be noted that most of the
professional staff (especially at more senior levels) have
no post-high school (full-time) education, and none of
the staff excluding the President have university degrees.
The senior staff (again excluding the President) are
people who have spent most of their working life with SY
FLIA (or the organisation which under another name formed
the core of the present organisation [10] before SY was
formed by the amalgamation of several smaller FLIAs in
1961). They are promotees.   However, at senior levels
they have all had some in-service training, and have
passed an examination (set by the provincial administration) to pass from grade 4 to grade 3.

TABLE 3.1
SY FLIA Staff

	Admin-istration	Technical	Other	Total
Professional staff	38	61 *	-	99
Employees	24	54	-	78
- salaried (permanent)	10	39	-	49
- daily wage (temporary)	14	15	-	29
Patrollers (daily wage)	-	-	109	109
Total	62	115	109	286

* includes President and Manager, both of whom have
  technical backgrounds.

THE BUDGET

To round out this introduction we need to note a
few points about SY's budget (Table 3.3).   About 79
percent of its ordinary (non-capital) revenue came from
water charges in 1977 (72 percent for all FLIAs).   On
the expenditure side, 28 percent of SY's ordinary
expenditure went on general administrative expenses
(salaries alone, 23 percent);   for all FLIAs the average
was the same.   Another 38 percent of SY's expenditure
went on operation, repair and maintenance (43 percent
for all FLIAs).   Both SY and all FLIAs put together
operate with a small surplus of revenue over expenditure.

ASSESSMENT OF WATER CHARGES

Water charges in South Korea have no connection with
quantity of water used, but are based on a division of
operating and capital costs between the beneficiaries.
All recurrent expenditure has to be covered by the FLIA's
earned income (mainly water charges).   The charges also
have to cover a proportion of construction costs.   The

TABLE 3.2

SY FLIA Number of Staff by Grade, and Whether Administrator (A) or Technician (T)

Unit or Position	1a	1b	2 A	2 T	3 A	3 T	4 A	4 T	5 A	5 T	Permanent Employee A	Permanent Employee T	Temporary Employee A	Temporary Employee T	Canal Patroller	Total (excluding patrollers)
President	1															1
Manager		1														1
Administration Bur:Head			1													1
Personnel & Admin Secn:					1		1		2		2	4	2	3		15
Budget Secn					1		1		2		1	3				8
Finance Secn					1			3			1	1				6
Management Bur:Head			1													1
Canal O & Ag Aff Secn						1		1	2			1				5
Maintenance Secn						1		5	3		1	1				11
Land Devt Bur:Head				1												1
Eng Affairs Secn					1				2					1		4
Land Devt & Consold[n] Secn					1			2	3			3	1			10
Field Station Section I						1	2	1	1	2		1	2	4	12	14
Field Station Bureau II:				1												1
II Admin Secn					1		1		2		1	4			n.k.	9
II Technical Secn						1		1		6		7		5	n.k.	20
Field Station Section III						1	1	1	2		1	3			n.k.	9
IV							1	1	1	1		2			5	6
V						1	1	1	1	2	2	2	1		n.k.	11
VI							2	1	2	1		5			n.k.	11
VII						1	1	2	1			5			n.k.	10
VIII						1	1	1	1	3		3	1		n.k.	11
Reservoir Watch Off IX								1				1	1			3
Ag. Machinery Off X					1		1		2		1	3				8
	1	1	2	2	7	8	13	19	16	30	10	36	14	15	109	177

TABLE 3.3

SY FLIA, and All FLIAs, Financial Statement, 1977 (000,000 won)

	SY	Total		SY	Total
ORDINARY REVENUE			PROJECT REVENUE		
Water charge	713.9	22,957.2	New irrigation		
Non operating gain			facility	1,162.6	30,940.9
and commission	54.9	2,400.7	Facility Improve-		
Loan	–	842.2	ment	–	2,119.6
Transfer	23.8	)	Rehabilitation	–	673.0
Carried over	94.9	)5,770.4	Land consolidation	712.4	11,529.1
Others	20.9	)	Farmland improve-		
Total	908.4	31,970.6	ment	–	131.9
			Total	1,875.0	45,394.6
EXPENDITURE					
General Admin.:			EXPENDITURE		
Salary	185.2		New irrigation		
Others	42.3		facility	1,055.2	28,686.9
Sub-total	227.5	8,062.4	Facility improve-		
Operation & Main-			ment	–	1,518.0
tenance of assets			Rehabilitation	–	668.3
(buildings)	58.5	1,519.5	Land consolidation	664.7	11,171.5
Side project formu-			Farmland improve-		
lation	13.9	389.1	ment	–	120.9
Project cost:			Total	1,719.9	42,165.6
O & M	125.3				
Repair	169.9		TOTAL REVENUE	2,783.0	
Farm practice					
improvement	14.2		TOTAL EXPENDITURE	2,525.3	
Sub-total	309.4	12,315.6			
Reserve:					
Depreciation	71.8				
Retirement allowance	35.6				
Others	17.3				
Sub-total	124.7	2,146.6			
Loan repayment:					
Long-term	53.7				
Other	17.6				
Sub-total	71.4	3,787.1			
Other	189.9				
Total	805.4	28,410.4			
Balance	102.6	3,560.2			

Source: Agricultural Development Corporation, 1978.

Notes: 1. Totals may not add correctly due to rounding errors.
2. Project cost O & M refers to running expenses, weeding, etc;
'repair' refers to rehabilitation work.
3. Retirement allowance refers to the lump sum paid to staff on
retirement.

government provides a 70 percent subsidy for
construction projects (reservoirs, main conveyance
and drainage structures), leaving 30 percent to be
repaid by irrigators, for which cheap long-term loans
(3.5 percent interest over thirty-five years) are
available from the state. Cost of land development
(levelling, rectangularisation, field channels) are
the third component which water charges have to cover.
The state provides 71 percent of land development cost,
leaving the irrigator to pay 29 percent, of which half
can be (and often is) in labour time.

Costs are divided according to the principle of
net benefit: farmers who gain more from the project pay
a higher proportion of costs than those who gain less.
Thus, the charge is assessed per hectare: two hectares
are liable to twice as much as one, other things being
equal. However the per hectare charge varies between
farmers, for several reasons.

First, each independent irrigation system within a
FLIA is treated as a separate accounting unit, so as to
apply the principle of linking costs with direct
beneficiaries. Each accounting unit is called an
irrigation 'district'. In SY FLIA the four big
reservoirs are taken as a single district, and the
thirteen small reservoirs constitute twelve irrigation
districts. The farmers under the small reservoirs have
to pay a portion of the general administrative expenses
of the whole FLIA; but do not contribute to, for
example, the capital and operating expenses of pump
stations outside of their irrigation systems, whereas
the farmers under the four reservoirs have to share the
expense of each pump station in the command area of the
four reservoirs (because this constitutes a single
district). This then is one source of variation between
farmers in the per hectare rate. 11

Second, cross-cutting the classification into
irrigation districts is a classification of each hectare
into four grades according to its use before the present
facilities were constructed. Grade 1 is land which was
forest or river; grade 2, 'upland', that is, cultivated
but unirrigated; 3, paddy land of inferior quality;
4, paddy land of superior quality. The principle is
that grade 1 land should pay the most, and grade 4 the
least; very roughly, each grade should pay ten
kilograms of rice per hectare less than the preceding
grade. This produces variation in water charges within
each district.

Third, in areas within a district where the water
supply is recognised to be substantially worse than
average, the farmers pay 30 percent less than the
average charge for their grade(s) of land in that
district.

Fourth, farmers whose average yield is less than

two tons per hectare will be given a reduction in water
charges, according to a nationally uniform scale set by
the Ministry of Agriculture: between 2.0 and 1.5 tons,
a 30 percent reduction, between 1.5 and 1.0 tons, 70
percent, and less than 1.0 ton, the farmer pays nothing.

In the latter, we see the principle that those who
have normal or better than normal yields should pay for
those who have very much worse than normal yields.

The calculation of the actual amount to be paid by
each farmer is an enormously complex, time-consuming
operation. Because the FLIA tries to avoid borrowing
to meet a current account deficit, the more reductions
there are for some the higher the charges for others
must be. The calculations are made by the staff of
the Finance section over a period of several weeks,
using electronic pocket calculators and abacuses
(the latter being preferred).

In terms of the average for each grade of land,
the following table gives the figures for the four
reservoir district:

TABLE 3.4
SY FLIA Average Water Charges in the Four
Reservoir System, 1977.

Grade	(1)	(2)	(3)	(4)	Total
Area (ha)	44	511	3992	3094	7641
Average water charge per ha. (000 won)	78.7	74.8	72.6	71.2	72.4

Between the districts the difference in charges can
be substantial; in 1977, for example, the average for
the four reservoir districts was 72,390 won per hectare,
while four of the twelve other districts had average
charges of less than 60,000 won per hectare. [12]

THE IRRIGATION PROBLEM

SY's area does not experience one of the most familiar
canal irrigation problems elsewhere in the world, the
'tail-end problem' - the failure to deliver to tail-end
areas a water supply adequate enough in timing and
amount to permit normal yields. Indeed, yield loss
over the whole irrigated area due to water stress seems
to be very small.

The problem, rather, is the cost of providing the
water supply and the other services. A rough comparison
with costs in Taiwan [13] suggests SY farmers (and South
Korean farmers more generally) are paying water charges
of the same order of magnitude as Taiwanese farmers, but
for only one irrigated crop rather than two or more.

Such comparisons are problematic, however (especially because Taiwan's Irrigation Associations provide a different range of services to those of the FLIAs), and a more sensible standard may be the likely costs of alternative methods of supply. By this criterion it seems clear that alternatives are available which would save substantially on costs, without causing yield losses due to water stress. We come to these in the next chapter. A second problem is the poor standard of maintenance, perhaps due to inadequate spending. A third problem, related to the first, is the absence of concern amongst those responsible for managing the system with improving its operation, other than by expensive 'hardware' improvement (in particular, lining the conveyance channels). Indeed, remarkably little data has been collected on key parameters of the project or its environment, which could provide a basis for calculating how to improve canal operation. Such data is not thought to be important. On the other hand, the FLIA staff do spend much of their time collecting and processing information bureaucratically, and the degree of formalisation of organisation and procedures is impressive; but the codifications and information have more to do with the FLIA's relations with the government than with its activities for the farmers. To the latter, relatively little attention is devoted.

NOTES

1. SY is a pseudonym.
2. This is confirmed by experiments done in 1970-71 (not in SY area), which showed that normal groundwater temperature reduces yields by about 20 per cent compared to normal surface water application (Wook Dong Han, 1972.)
3. Figures for the county with the largest area in the system (out of five) include non-irrigated as well as irrigated land. For 1976 they are:

Total		Farm size (ha), % of total						
		0.5		0.5-1.0		1.0 - 3.0		3.0	
No.	Area ha.	No.	Area	No.	Area	No.	Area	No.	Area
18,471	20,534	28	10	25	18	42	59	4	14

4. Near towns, however, the proportion of tenanted land is higher.

5. MAF,Agricultural Development Corporation, 1978,
Table 20.

6. These figures are rough orders of magnitude
only; the ranges indicate what most farmers are within.
The figures are based on (a) conversations with several
local farmers about their own and their neighbours'
practices, (b) the impressions of the head of Rural
Guidance Office in one of the counties, (c) the results
of a survey of sixteen out of sixty-six USAID projects
in several parts of South Korea, involving 44 villages,
220 households, to investigate, amongst other things,
fertiliser use before and after full-scale irrigated
land development (MAF, Agriculture Development
Corporation, 1976). The latter gives, for 1975,
averages of 420 kg/ha for chemical fertiliser, 8,250
kg/ha for compost, and 390 kg/ha and 8,220 kg/ha, for
land after development under HYVs and traditional
varieties, respectively. The associated rice yield
figures are 5,050 kg/ha, and 4,040 kg/ha, respectively.

7. MAF, Agricultural Development Corporation, 1978
Tables 11 and 21.

8. Impressionistic estimates of head of Rural
Guidance Office and head of Agricultural Affairs Section,
SY FLIA.

9. The southern provinces of South Korea tend to
be more unequal, with a larger proportion of poor
people, than the provinces further north.

10. This earlier organisation, called the X
Irrigation Association, was formed in 1953. It had only
a few small reservoirs, most of its area being fed from
river diversion supplemented by groundwater.

11. The principle of having beneficiaries pay is
carried to the point where no transfer of funds is
allowed between the 'districts' within the same FLIA.
This means that if an accident occurs in a particular
project and emergency work is needed, the work may be
held up if the reserve fund of that district is not
currently large enough to bear the cost. The President
of the FLIA has no discretionary power in this respect.
The SY staff think this restriction harms the
effectiveness of the FLIAs; but the government's
proposed irrigation reform (Chapter 7) makes no
provision to change it.

12. Gilbert Levine (personal communication)
comments that this difference of approximately 20
percent in rates is not especially large compared to
rate differences within the same Irrigation Association
in Taiwan and the United States.

13. Based on figures for Taiwan in an unpublished
paper by Anthony Bottrall, Overseas Development
Institute, London.

4
The Organisation
of Main Functions

This chapter describes the way the main functions are
carried out: those of water delivery, agricultural
extension, and maintenance of structures. (Land
development is not considered.) [1]   The emphasis is on
the first, on the way the irrigation system is operated
and water delivered when needed. Our interest is to
know how it is ensured that the required amount of
irrigation water is delivered to the fields at the
required time, over an area of nearly 11,500 hectares.
(For convenience I restrict the discussion to the
structures and operation of the canal systems fed from
the four main reservoirs, which irrigate 9,400 hectares.)
That the system must do this effectively is suggested by
the increase in average yields of rice in the FLIA's area
over the past 10 years (at least) to the present
average of five tons per hectare. This suggests (though
does not necessarily imply) that over virtually the
whole area in recent years, yield loss due to water
stress is slight.

STRUCTURES FOR WATER DELIVERY AND DRAINAGE

We begin with a description of the physical
structures, to gauge, if very approximately, the level
of water control they make possible. Details are shown
in Tables 4.1 and 4.2 for the reservoirs, canals, and
pump stations. Notice that of the canal systems from the
four main reservoirs the longest is thirty-six
kilometres, the shortest twenty-seven kilometres, and
their maximum carrying capacity ranges from 3.8 to 6.3
cubic metres per second (136 and 225 cubic feet per
second). The altitude drop is from about 50-60 metres
above sea level at the reservoirs, to 5-15 metres at
the tail-ends. Most of the irrigated area of the four
reservoirs lies in a narrow strip rarely more than two
kilometres wide on either side of the river which feeds
into and issues from the reservoir. The canals snake
along the base of the hills on either side of the
river, and irrigation water flows down from the canals

TABLE 4.1 SY Reservoirs and Canals

Reservoir & Canal System	No.	Cultivable Command Area ha.	Catchment Area ha.	Reservoir Effective Capacity ha.m.	Main Canals		Branch Canals			Outlet Gates(2)	Cross Regulating Gates(3)	Discharge Gates(4)
					Total Length kms.	(1) Number	Total Length kms.	Number(1)	Maximum Discharge m3/sec			
Kum Kwang	1	2,254	4,830	1,055	36	1	5	2	4.3			
Ko Sam	1	3,518	7,100	1,502	32	2	19	4	5.8			
Kae Hueng	1	2,277	5,300	1,069	34	3	8	6	3.8	n.a.	n.a.	n.a.
Li Dong	1	3,435	9,300	1,720	27	2	11	4	6.3			
Other	13	2,223	6,651	1,026	72	18	34	20	-			
Total	17	13,707	33,181	6,372	201	26	77	36		794	11	24

Notes: 1. The distinction between main canals and branch canals is illustrated in Map 3.1. On Ko Sam canal, A and B are classed as main canals, C and D as branch canals. Not all the branch canals listed in the table are shown on the map.

2. Outlet gates include approximately 36 gates from main canal to branch canal.

3. Cross regulating gates are across the direction of flow in a main canal.

4. Discharge gates are for the purpose of discharging canal water into rivers or drains.

TABLE 4.2

SY Pump Stations

H.P. per Pump Station	Number of Pump Stations	Total H.P.	Number of Pumps	Irrigable Area ha.	Capacity m^3/sec
16-99	12	446	20	884	2.17
100-500	7	1,620	14	3,106	8.19
> 500	1	2,150	4	2,131	4.77
Total	20	4,216	38	6,121	15.13

towards the river. Because of the narrow width of the
area between canal and river, the canal systems are made
up predominantly of the main trunk alone. The 129
kilometres of the four main canals are supplemented by
only forty-three kilometres of branch canals, each
averaging only 2.7 kilometres. Hence while the variety
of water sources in the SY system is large, each canal
is straightforward as a conveyance structure.[2] The
canals are unlined, except in a few weak places.

By South Asian standards the density of control
structures is high. There are eleven cross-gates for
regulating main canal flows, or one per eleven
kilometres, and water gauges in the main canal every
three or four kilometres. The density of gated outlets
from canal to fields is especially high: one gated
outlet per fourteen hectares overall, and in land
development areas (8,600 hectares out of 11,200) the
density is still higher, roughly one to eight to ten
hectares. The gates are of concrete, with a steel
shutter raised and lowered on a spindle.

All gates and other adjustable control structures
(except the main reservoir gates) are operated manually,
without motorised assistance. In virtually all cases
there are no measuring devices to monitor the amount of
water flowing through the gate. Below the gated outlet
are pipe outlets from the lateral to the fields, which
are blocked with mud and stones when the water in the
lateral is not wanted on the fields. The laterals
are unlined.

In the area which has been 'developed' the fields
are arranged in a grid pattern. Each field is
connected directly to a water supply channel at one end
and a drainage channel at the other. Average field
size is about 0.3 - 0.4 hectares. (Fields may be

subdivided to accommodate differences between field
size and ownership size.)   Elsewhere (and everywhere
before land development) irrigation takes place from
field-to-field.

With rainfall likely to be intense and with land
near the rivers being relatively flat, drainage is
important.   Both within and outside the land development area are major drainage canals, in addition to the
rivers themselves.   The drainage canals are often
linked to irrigation canals either directly or by
low-lift pump, so that water in the drains can be re-used
for irrigation.   The irrigation canals have a total of
twenty-four discharge gates for releasing water in the
canals into the drains and rivers at times when the
level in the canals rises dangerously high.   Flood
protection works are the responsibility of the
provincial administration to build and maintain (not of
the FLIA).   Most of the SY area is well protected. [3]

Finally, the twenty pump stations are for lifting
surface water from rivers, canals, drains - rather than
groundwater.   They tend to be near tail-end areas of
the canal systems.   Their irrigable area is included in
the irrigable area of the reservoirs (Tables 4.1 and 4.2).
Most of the pump stations (fourteen out of twenty) are
for supplementing canal flows in the same area; that
is, only seven out of twenty lift water to where it
could not physically flow by gravity alone.   This
important point will be returned to.

In short, though very little of the water
distribution network is lined, the control structures
(especially gates) are sufficiently dense to permit a
relatively high (by comparison with South and Southeast
Asian publicly-owned canals) level of control over
water to be exercised by the canal managers.

I am not in a position to evaluate the adequacy
of the physical structures in terms of design, construction and maintenance.   However, one point can be made.
It seems (though no precise information is available)
that many of the gated outlets are out of action.   The
staff of one section, with ninety gated outlets for
770 irrigated hectares, estimated that 'about one third'
of the gates were not working in the sense that they
could not be moved up and down to increase or diminish
the flow through the outlet.   We noted earlier that
many observers of South Korean irrigation have commented
on the often poor state of maintenance.

CROPPING CALENDAR

The last frost is in April, the first frost in
October.   The irrigation season starts in April and ends
in September.   About 20 March the ploughing to prepare

the rice paddies begins. Seedling nurseries are
started about 10 April or soon after, when water from
the canal arrives. (The seedbeds are normally covered
with vinyl sheeting, to reduce risk of frost damage.)
The seedlings are in the nurseries for forty days or more.
Transplanting begins about 20 May and continues until
about 10 June, with the optimal period (in terms of
yields) generally around 25-30 May; but some
transplanting may still be going on up to about 25 June
(beyond this date, the loss of yield is serious). This
period from May to June is the time of peak irrigation
water use. The period in the field is about one
hundred and twenty days with the new varieties.
Harvesting begins 20-25 September, and continues until
late October. The frosts likely from late October
onwards set a constraint on when the harvesting must
be finished.

Until recently the SY FLIA, following the lead of
the Ministry of Agriculture, urged farmers to grow a
second crop of barley on the paddy lands during the
winter season. But little barley was in fact grown, and
the FLIA has now given up its promotion efforts. If
barley is grown, it must be planted in early October
(12 October at the latest); and will not come to
harvest until 10-20 June. To grow barley thus means
that the transplanting of paddy has to be delayed (the
land must first be prepared for paddy after the barley
is cleared off the fields); this may cause some
reduction in paddy yields. It also means that the
harvesting of paddy is more concentrated than otherwise,
at a time when labour is in any case in short supply.
Most of the double cropped area (19 percent of the total)
is grown under vegetables for the Seoul and local
markets.

RULES AND ROLES OF WATER DELIVERY

The reservoirs are open from 10 April to 30
September. During this period the whole canal system
is normally open all the time except when heavy rains
make the water unwanted. When the farmers want it,
water flows continuously from lateral-to-each-plot in
the land development areas, and continuously from-plot
to-plot in the other areas. That is, the rule of
water delivery is continuous flow. There is no attempt
to save water by opening and shutting some gates in
rotation, or by having each plot take water from the
lateral in rotation. Only during the 1978 drought,
described as the worst in over 20 years, was a slight
degree of rotational delivery attempted - and soon
abandoned. I describe what happened shortly.

We would expect from knowledge of irrigation
systems elsewhere that the roles, procedures and

communications facilities associated with a continuous
flow delivery rule would be relatively simple compared
to those on systems using rotational delivery. [4]   The
arrangements at SY are indeed organisationally simple,
and simpler in practice than in principle, though the
communications technology is relatively sophisticated.
In principle the arrangements are as follows:

On the early morning patrol the patrollers read the
main gauges in their area (normally only two or three)
and report the readings to the Field Station (by phone
or in person).   These readings are then sent to the
Canal Operation and Agricultural Affairs Section at HQ.
(From now on I refer to this section by the title which
the SY staff give it: Agricultural Affairs, the 'Canal
Operation' part - significantly - being dropped.)   The
Field Station also communicates to HQ the previous
twenty four hours' rainfall.

This communication is by radio: SY has its own
transmitter and receiver system linking HQ and field
officers, and officers are supplied with portable sets
to take with them on visits to the command area.   (In
the case of some of the small reservoirs, communication
is by phone.)

The head of Agricultural Affairs inspects the
readings before passing them on to the Manager with
his suggestions about what action should be taken.
The Manager passes the information on to the President
with his own view.   The President makes the decisions,
and the orders come down the hierarchy, eventually
reaching the patrollers in time for their next round.

Once or twice weekly the patrollers meet at their
Station office to discuss difficulties or queries with
the staff, particularly the head of Station and the head
of the Technical sub-section.   At these meetings
verbal instructions are given to the patrollers on what
they are to do before the next meeting.

Each member of the Station office (excluding the
head, but including all other staff, administrators as
well as technicians) has responsibility for supervising
one or two patrollers.   At least once a day he must go
out (on a FLIA motorcycle) to the patroller's area
during the time the patroller is supposed to be on duty
and check that he is there and doing what he is supposed
to be doing.   He need not meet the patroller, nothing
has to be counter-signed.   He must simply see that the
patroller is on the job, and has then to put his
signature stamp in a special register and indicate which
out of five kinds of activities the patroller was mainly
engaged in (weeding; desilting; removing refuse such
as vinyl sheeting, bottles; lifting and shutting water
gates; and 'other').   The first three are specified
by location.   On the basis of these signature stamps
the patroller is paid his daily wage (at month's end).

In _practice_, the arrangements for the supervision
of the patrollers do operate more or less as prescribed.
It is a common sight to see a Field Station office
member cruising through the command area on a FLIA
motorcycle going to or from the place where the patroller
is working.   It is not an onerous task and provides
relief from the office routine.   (In rain neither the
patroller nor the supervisor are expected to be on the
job, unless there is risk of flooding or breaching.)
The registers showing the supervisor's signature and the
type of work the patroller was doing that day are,
indeed, actually filled in and sent to HQ - but in
almost all cases the work is identified as 'lifting and
shutting water gates'.   This is also the safest of the
five categories to choose from the supervisor's point
of view, since even if he surreptitiously doesn't go
to the area that day he can be sure that the patroller
did some adjusting of gates - and even if not there is
no evidence that he did not, as there is if the
patroller is stated as having done, say, weeding at
point x.   Further, the weekly or twice weekly
meetings of Station staff with patrollers are often
cancelled;   or more exactly, they occur only if and
when a patroller or two or three come to the Station
office and ask advice.   Meetings of all the patrollers
do however occur occasionally, when, for example, the
FLIA is especially anxious to promote the use of sprays
against pests and diseases.   Then, as part of the wider
campaign, the patrollers will be called in to the
Station office and briefed on what to tell the farmers
(the briefings are based on Ministry of Agriculture
booklets).   But in practice, the choice of what they
do, when, is normally left to them.   The supervisor,
and any other staff going through the area, will keep
an eye out for things that need to be done, and will
pass this on to the patroller - generally by way of
suggestion rather than as an authoritative command.
Indeed, the arrangements for controlling and monitoring
the patrollers are marked by a lack of emphasis on
hierarchy.   In interpersonal relations between patrollers
and staff one sees, by South Asian standards, a remarkable lack of an authoritarian/subordinate manner. 5
   In practice, the patrollers have considerable
discretion to decide how to spend their time on the job,
and also have considerable autonomy in water delivery.
In practice, the rule of water delivery in normal times
could better be described as 'demand delivery' than as
'continuous flow' delivery;   for how much water goes to
different parts of the command area depends heavily on
what the farmers individually want.   As the patroller
bicycles past on one of his twice daily patrols (at
fairly fixed times) the farmers tell him - or shout to
him - that they want some more water down lateral x,

or that they want lateral y closed (after heavy rain).
He of course will often be able to anticipate water
needs from past experience, and does not always wait to
be asked to lower or shut the gates.   The point is
that the farmers in practice can, if they wish, have
much influence over how much water they get to their
fields, and when.   (Even when a shutter is closed,
the patroller closes the last few inches with mud and
stones, so that if only a few farmers want water they
can remove the obstacles themselves and may be able to
get what they want without asking the patroller to lift
the shutter.)   In practice, too, the patroller has the
decision about when to open and shut off the pump
station in his area.   Opening and shutting off the pump
has to be reported to the Station office;   but after,
rather than prior to doing so.
     In principle, then, the water delivery system
could be described as (a) supply-controlled, in the
sense that the personnel of the system, rather than the
individual users, control the allocation of water; (b)
centralised, in the sense that allocation decisions are
to be taken high up the administrative structure;   and
(c) based on continuous flow rather than rotational
delivery.   In practice the system is normally (a)
quasi-demand-controlled, in the sense that individual
users have much influence over how much water they get
and when, and (b) decentralised in the sense that
effective decision-making lies with the patroller and
the users.   In practice, the President and Manager of
the FLIA only have an active directing role in drought
periods;   and even then, their concern is primarily with
water releases from the reservoir - with the single
decision of how much water to release each day, not with
its allocation throughout the area;   and the reservoir
decision is effectively taken by the head of Agricultural
Affairs and passed up to the Manager and President for
approval.
     Distribution of water below the outlet is in the
hands of the farmers themselves. Only in (rare) cases
of dispute over water might the patroller become
involved. Routine water distribution between fields
is carried out individually;   there is no attempt at
concerted action, nor are 'common irrigators' employed
to distribute water to each field in turn. [6]

OPERATIONAL INFORMATION

     In practice, the irrigation system is operated with
very little quantitative data.   Some gauges are in
practice read daily and the results communicated to HQ,
where they are normally glanced at by the head of
Agricultural Affairs, then the Manager and President -
all three must put their signature stamp to the

document. But the staff of Agricultural Affairs warned me that they did not use the gauge reports except to get a very approximate idea of what was happening. 'These agricultural affairs are best done by eye', said one. The main source of information about what is happening in the command area is the patrollers and their supervisors out on their bicycles and motorbikes; their information is communicated verbally, and generally not recorded on paper. Not surprisingly, the painted scale on the main gauges (one per three to four kilometres of main canal, none in the branch canals) is in many cases unreadably faint; and the gauge register at HQ shows many blank spaces - commonly a third or more of the gauges will have no daily entry, even during a severe drought like that of May-June 1978. Just how little reliance is placed on quantitative data is illustrated by the absence of a scale linking the <u>level</u> on the gauge which measures reservoir releases, with flow. That is to say, the staff have - surprisingly - no way of readily knowing how much water is leaving the reservoirs. The same absence of any scale converting the level of water leaving the reservoir with flow has been found on all nine projects visited by a foreign irrigation engineer working in South Korea. In all these projects, as at SY, the staff could only calculate the flow by searching through old records to find the (original) dimensions of the canal, and making the calculation afresh. This strongly suggests that the unimportance of precise information on water quantities which we have seen at SY is characteristic of South Korean canal irrigation management generally. At SY FLIA, and presumably elsewhere, the canal managers make use of largely implicit rules-of-thumb linking level at the discharge gauge with level in the reservoir and time of year (time of year being used to guess future irrigation demand and rainfall).

Since there is a good alternative communication system, given by the frequent movement of (the numerous) staff throughout the command area and by the radio link between HQ and Station offices, and since the canals are in any case short, it is not surprising that the gauge reports are unimportant in the system of water control. For the same reasons it is perhaps not surprising that no data is collected on the time of transplanting in different parts of the canal systems.

It is more surprising however that little information is available on key characteristics of the project environment and the physical structures. For example, (1) the staff do not have information on the soil types in the command area - nor do they have more than a rudimentary working knowledge in their heads ('sandier towards the rivers'). (2) No experiments

have been made to determine even roughly percolation
rates (in millimetres of water per day), either as an
average for the whole area or for sub-areas.   (3) No
reliable information is available on conveyance losses.
The head of Agricultural Affairs section said 20 percent,
then changed the figure to 15 percent - but was not
sure whether it referred to losses in the main system
only   or losses from reservoir to field.   He said the
figure came from a training course, not from SY
specifics.   His subordinates did not know, nor did the
head of Maintenance.   (4) There has been no identification of how much water is used in the various stages of
crop growth, in local conditions.   (5) At field office
level (as well as at HQ) the staff tend not to know,
nor to have readily available, information on such basic
characteristics as the length of main and branch canals
in their section, depth of groundwater, number of gates,
the area irrigated from each outlet, number and location
of broken gates. [8]
    The head of Maintenance Section reported that on
the training course he had attended the previous year he
had been taught methods of computing irrigation requirement, conveyance losses, discharge flows, and had
attempted to make some of the calculations for SY's
systems on his return.   He had given up, however, because
of the lack of basic data more up-to-date than that
given in the original plans.

WATER SUPPLY

    The (unsurprising) reason for loose control over
water by the system managers is that in most years, for
most of the season, water is not short.   The earlier
discussion on water requirement and supply in South
Korean paddy agriculture needs to be recalled here.
In terms of long-run averages, there is a monthly surplus
of rainfall over crop need during the growing season,
except in May (a small deficit).   Irrigation is needed
to offset downward fluctuations around the monthly
averages;   and drainage (the structures for which are
part of the irrigation system) is needed to carry away
surface run-off and prevent flooding.
    For reasons implicit in the foregoing, it is
difficult to make any reliable calculation of the water
supply available in the SY system in relation to the
water requirements of the paddy grown under it.   The
relevant information does not exist, and in any case
the interlinking of systems (such as small reservoirs
which feed their own command area but also feed into a
main canal), and the use of riverwater and drainage
water makes the calculation complex.   Nevertheless, a
highly simplified calculation for the four main
reservoirs (the details of which can be left to a

footnote) suggests that all four reservoirs fail by
only a small margin to store (effectively) sufficient
water to meet the irrigation requirement in the worst
in ten years' drought. [9]

However, it is more instructive to look at what
actually happenen in 1978, a year described by FLIA
staff as the worst drought they have known (in at
least twenty years).

SUPPLYING WATER IN THE DROUGHT OF 1978

April 1978 brought only 11 mm of rain in the SY
area, May 32 mm, compared with a 1970-78 average for
these months of 111 mm and 100 mm respectively. [10]
This meant that from early April onwards much greater
reliance was placed on irrigation water than in a normal
year.   Figures 4.1 and 4.2 show rainfall for 1978
compared to other years;   Figure 4.3 shows the drawdown
in reservoir storage in 1978 compared to other years
(for one of the four main reservoirs only).   By the end
of May, when the demand for water for transplanting is
heavy, this reservoir (like the others) was already down
to about 20 percent of its effective storage - and heavy
rain would not normally come until early July.   What was
the response?

The pump stations were of course worked to the full
where they could still draw water.

There was also some discussion between the HQ staff
in charge of water allocation (the President, Manager,
and head of Agricultural Affairs) of introducing a
rudimentary rotation between sections of the main canals.
On Kum Kwang canal, for instance, it was decided to use
the cross-gate half way down the canal (at the point
marked S on Map 3.1) to close the bottom half for four
to five days at a time, and then close all the upper
gates for roughly the same period.   This was the full
extent of the 'rotation' they aimed to adopt.   But
after discussion with the Station heads they decided
to attempt not even this much, on the grounds that
because the soils towards the rivers in the bottom half
tended to be relatively sandy and permeable, water
would be needed urgently after only three days;   and in
the flat areas near the rivers, it might take seven days
for tail-end farmers to get water from the time it first
began to flow again in their branch or lateral, if all
the upstream farmers wanted to take it first.   Their
paddy would be destroyed.

The staff of one Station decided to try a rotation
within their Section.   Their situation was especially
serious since they were the effective tail-end of the
canal (the one Section further down had a pump station
by means of which some of its water requirement could
be supplied from the river).   The staff tried to divert

60

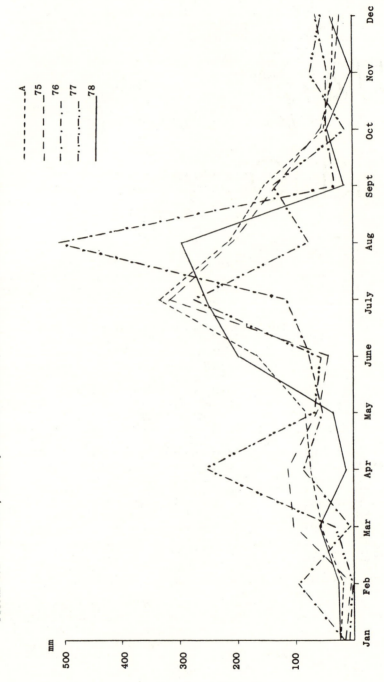

FIGURE 4.1 SY FLIA, Monthly Rainfall Totals, 1975-78 and Long-term Average (A)

Source: nearby state metereological office

FIGURE 4.2 SY FLIA, 10 Day Rainfall Totals, 1975-8 Irrigation Seasons

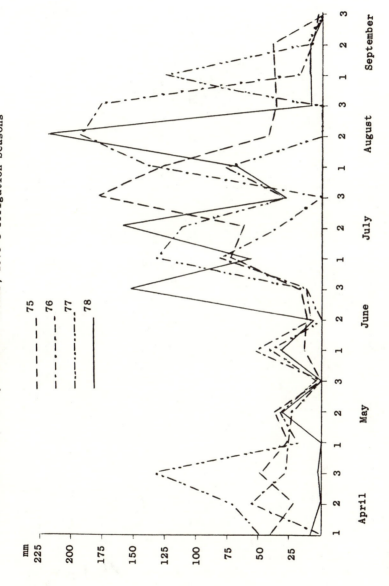

Source: FLIA records

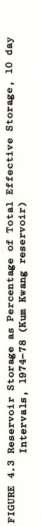
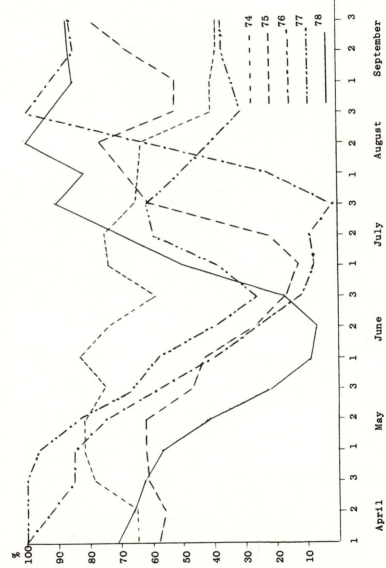

FIGURE 4.3 Reservoir Storage as Percentage of Total Effective Storage, 10 day Intervals, 1974-78 (Kum Kwang reservoir)

all the water discharged into their Section to the five
short branch canals in turn. But after the first two
branches had been fed in this way they gave up, because
even with the rotation water flowed only a short way
down each channel during its open turn, such was the
demand from farmers close to the outlets.

In any case, the water coming into their Section
was decreasing rapidly, and by the end of May had
ceased altogether. By that time the staff (like the
staff elsewhere) were concentrating their whole
attention on providing farmers with alternative means
of getting water - particularly plastic pipes for
transporting water lifted from rivers and underground
infiltration galleries. They also helped farmers buy
small portable pumps to attach to two-wheeled tractors,
and the FLIA itself made a number of pumps available.
Throughout the period of mid May to the end of June the
staff were rarely in the office - all attention was
directed to assisting farmers somehow to get water.
Many farmers made their own arrangments to buy water
from the owner of a tubewell, and the water might have
to be piped distances of several hundred metres, in a
few cases, kilometres, to where it was needed.

That despite the drought the paddies suffered little
water stress is suggested by three points: first,
average yields were reported as higher than in previous
years other than 1977 (a record year). [11] Even if the
actual average yield figure was lower than the official
figure (and since the figures are collected by FLIA
officials there may be an upward bias), much of the
reduction, according to both farmers and officials,
was due to a severe disease outbreak later in the season,
not directly to water stress.   Second, the total area
which produced less than 2000 kilograms per hectare of
rice (the owners of which were therefore entitled to
a reduction on water charges) was assessed at only 286
hectares out of over 11,000. [12] Third, as far as one
can tell (this is a subject on which evidence is difficult
to get) the farmers did not conflict with each other or
with the FLIA staff over water. The staff of the
Section described earlier did report that eight irate
women from a village at the tail-end of a branch canal
marched into the Field Station office while the staff
were holding a meeting, and demanded to know why they
could not get water from the reservoir, if, as they
had just heard, farmers in the Section upstream were
getting reservoir water. They would understand, they
said, if there was no water in the reservoir to be had,
but the fact that the upstream people were getting
some meant that there was water to be had, and they
should get some too. Whereupon the staff offered   to
help them the next day to carry water by hand from the
river to supplement the pumps, and the women went away

contrite; the next day the staff did as promised. Of course, the general absence of conflict may reflect, instead, the wider distribution of power in the political system: the sanctions against public 'beyond the village' expressions of conflict may be so strong as to deter such expression even in the face of the risk of crop (and therefore livelihood) loss. The other evidence suggests that in this case, the explanation is rather that the farmers recognised there was no serious risk of water stress. They and the staff had to work long hours in order to keep the paddies irrigated, but there was not much danger of no water being available. It is worth noting, finally, that no attempt was made to mobilise other sections of the population, such as students, military, or other government officials, to help out; this was deemed unnecessary. [13]

The FLIA gave limited help to farmers in meeting the additional private cost of irrigation. Where farmers bought water from private tubewell or low-lift pump owners the FLIA granted them a 30 percent reduction in the water charge per hectare they would otherwise have had to pay. Where farmers bought plastic piping and fuel for pump engines, the FLIA gave them the cost of the fuel and the piping (but made no contribution to additional labour costs). The total additional cost spent on fighting the drought is estimated at eighty-four million won, or about 10 percent of the FLIA's savings fund; the government gave no help.

This account of water supply during the drought brings out one major characteristic of canal operation at SY; the absence of plans for changing water distribution policies under different degrees of water shortage. This is consistent with the absence of operational information we have already noted, and contrasts sharply with accounts of canal operation in Taiwan (and also Spain and the United States). [14]

THE SUBSTITUTES FOR IMPROVED MANAGEMENT

The account of the 1978 drought suggests that even in a severe drought the SY area is not short of water, because of the availability - at higher cost - of water from outside the normal sources. The fact that one gets no hint of bribery in water supply, or of farmers breaking gates open, or even just lifting the shutter on their own account, all of which are standard practices on Indian irrigation systems, points to the same conclusion, though there are certainly also cultural and political elements in the different response.

Other systems in South Korea will of course vary in how much supplementary water can be supplied if necessary. What is common to all, according to informed sources, is that little attention has been and is being paid to canal operation ; nowhere, for example, are efforts being made to draw up plans for changing water distribution policies under different degrees of water shortage, or more specifically, to introduce rotational irrigation on a widespread scale (as in Taiwan) - despite clear evidence from Taiwan on the effectiveness of rotational irrigation in reducing water losses, increasing yield per hectare, and spreading water more equitably [15] (and indeed, some evidence from South Korea, produced in experiments sponsored by the national irrigation design and construction organisation, the Agricultural Development C orporation).[16]

Rather,to improve water supply to the fields attention is being concentrated on engineering solutions: increasing the storage capacity of reservoirs, or lining the canals, or putting in pump stations. The Manager of SY, for instance, said in response to a question about why they did not attempt rotational irrigation in 1978, that lining the canal with concrete was necessary before rotation could be done. He had been trying to persuade the government to give a subsidy for canal lining on the grounds of urgent need, but the government refused. And while long term loans were meant to be available for such purposes, in fact no loan funds were available. So he concluded that nothing could be done to alter the way they distributed water. It may indeed be necessary to enlarge the capacity of some of the physical structures before rotational irrigation down the length of a canal can be practised. The point, rather, is that the managers are calling for improved physical structures on the assumption that there is no need for their utilisation of those structures to change; for example, no pilot projects in rotational irrigation have been introduced. One strongly suspects that a good part of the reason for the lining solution is that the managers feel embarrassed to have earthen, and therefore crude and primitive, canals. Earthworks do not correspond to their idea of what a modern canal should look like, and their sense of their own dignity and importance, and even of their service to farmers, is correspondingly slighted.

Two members of the FLIA's staff, the Manager and head of Agricultural Machinery section, were recently included in a group of some fifteen FLIA staff from around the country sent for two weeks to look at irrigation in Taiwan. They returned impressed by how much of the Taiwanese systems had been lined, and enthusiastic to line more of the SY system; but did not <u>notice</u> the practices of intensive rotational delivery of water also used in Taiwan. Even more strikingly, the head of the Bureau in the Ministry of Agriculture which supervises the operation of all FLIAs in the country, himself an agricultural economist, also noticed only the engineering solutions to enhanced water supply on his recent trip to Taiwan. It was he who identified the three engineering solutions noted above; but he identified them as the only alternatives, omitting to mention the possibilities of increasing water use efficiencies through improved management.

Lining the canal is of course very expensive. The Agricultural Development Corporation estimates that the average cost in South Korean conditions for lining the main canal is about 20,000 won per metre of length, or 60 million won for a thirty kilometre canal.

The preferred solution at SY so far has been the pump station. All but three of the 20 pump stations were built after 1965, in response to increasing water demand from farmers. However, as mentioned, fourteen of the twenty pump stations are not essential for supplying their area; they are to supplement water that does or could flow through the canal. These fourteen account for almost half of the total command area of the pump stations, and over a quarter of the total horse power. Even a very rough estimate of the cost of supplying water by pump compared to the cost of supplying the same quantity through the canal is made hazardous by the absence of data. What can be said is that the average cost of the pump stations per cubic metre of pumped water in 1978 was about 0.25 won, and about the same up to the end of June 1979. Just under half the total average cost was for electricity and oil, and about half for wages. With the cost of labour and oil increasing rapidly (nearly three quarters of South Korea's electricity is produced from oil-thermal plants), the cost of pumped water can be expected to rise rapidly also. Just how this cost compares with the average cost of canal water is not known, but it seems clear that the cost of pumped water is several times greater, at the least, and that the cost difference is likely to rise for the foreseeable future. The Agricultural Development Corporation estimates that the average operational cost per hectare of a project fed entirely from lowlift pumps is about 47 percent greater than the operational cost per hectare of a reservoir-based system (but these cost estimates include all pump stations which are part of a reservoir system, as they are at SY, in the cost of the reservoir-based system, which means that the operational cost of a pure gravity-flow system would be lower).

In short, the pump station option looks as though it will become increasingly bad economics in the cases where water could physically flow to the area, while the water management option will become an even better option than

it is at present.   Yet in 1979 the staff of Songwhan
Section, whose response to the water shortage of 1978
was described earlier, were arguing strongly that they
must have a pump station built to supply the tail-end
part of their Section.

AGRICULTURAL EXTENSION

While the thirty staff engaged in canal operation
and agricultural affairs do not do much water <u>management</u>,
they do spend much of their time out in the command
area checking that water is flowing to where it is
supposed to go.   Even in a normal year they are
particularly busy at the time of transplanting - if
necessary getting down into the canals to move the water
along (and not only the patrollers, but the professional
staff as well).
Their other main activity is agricultural extension.[17]
In principle, the professional staff get regular in-
service training; they pass on relevant information to
the patrollers, the patrollers pass it to the farmers;
and the staff pass it directly to farmers' leaders,
the head of the farmers' association in each village
(to be discussed later). However, in practice, the
frequency of in-service training for professional staff
is very low (about once every six years per person,
for two weeks at a time, supplemented by occasional
morning lectures). The patrollers are generally small
or marginal farmers, who are often not amongst the
more respected farmers of their village and whose
extension efforts are therefore likely to be not taken
very seriously by others.   And the meetings between
Section staff and farmers' association leaders take
place, even in principle, only twice a year.
The extension staff have two main functions , in
practice: to help the ordinary government extension
service (the Rural Guidance Office of the ORD) in
promoting 'optimum' levels of inputs; and to help spot
outbreaks of pests and diseases and teach the farmers
how to fight them. As we saw in Chapter 2   the
government has placed heavy emphasis on the spread of
HYVs in its agricultural strategy since 1970. At first
it made HYVs economically attractive by a guaranteed
purchase price at higher-than-market-level, but since
the mid 1970s has reduced the subsidy to the point of
almost removing the economic incentive. (Non-HYVs
command a premium in the market because they are
considered more tasty,and farmers prefer to grow them
not only for this reason but also because HYVs are
more susceptible to disease and at similar levels of
inputs are thought to give little more yield than the
older varieties.) [18]   With little economic incentive
farmers are reluctant to adopt, and therefore (in the

government's eyes) must be persuaded or forced by other means. This puts a heavy responsibility on the extension service. The methods range from yield competitions carrying substantial prizes, through to outright coercion. We consider the details in the next chapter. Suffice it to note here that reinforcing the efforts of the ORD extension staff in spreading HYVs is meant to be an important part of the job of the Agricultural Affairs staff.

Once the planting has been finished, the main extension work is to watch for outbreaks of pests and diseases and help combat them. The FLIA has its own spray pumps which it rents out to farmers, and the staff give advice on how to use the pumps and what sprays to use. The sprays are bought by the farmers individually, through the NACF. Some years (since 1970) the FLIA hires a helicopter for aerial spraying, the cost being covered partly by government subsidy, the rest divided among the benefiting farmers according to acreage. After the bad virus attack on the higher yielding variety (nopung) that the government had promoted so vigorously in 1978, orders came down through the government hierarchy that the greatest care was to be taken that such an outbreak did not occur again. So as the 1979 post-transplanting season began, the SY staff inundated the area with banners and signs which exhorted, 'Exterminate pests and diseases, SY FLIA'. Across roads, on the sides of bridges and on badges worn by the SY staff, this slogan was emblazoned. (The biggest, most extravagant sign vaulted the gateway to the HQ building - with a certain irony, because few farmers ever go there.)

In addition to their disease and pest control function the extension staff keep records of land preparation in each Section, and compare the amount done every ten days during the preparation period with target amounts worked out in advance. The purpose is to enable them to spot places where land preparation for the transplanting is going slower than it should be and investigate the reasons. The same is done at harvesting time, to monitor the progress of the harvest. The fact that they do keep records of land preparation and harvesting throws into relief the fact noted earlier that they do not keep records of transplanting dates; yet if they were concerned with scheduling of water they would keep records of transplanting dates, so as to be prepared to adjust water supplies to each area in accordance with the sequence of water demand after the transplanting.

It is worth noting that the staff do not make the area measurement of land preparation and harvesting themselves. They ask a local farmer, generally the leader of the farmers' association, how much land was ploughed (or harvested) in his village in the past ten days, and add the totals. Similarly for the records of area under different paddy varieties (especially HYV and non-HYV); the villagers are asked to give a figure. This means both that this part of the job is not particularly onerous (as it would be if the staff had to make the measurements themselves); and that the figures are likely to be unreliable - which matters because these figures are sent to the Ministry of Agriculture to become part of the official national figures on, for example, the spread of HYVs. Village leaders know well the government's concern to push HYVs (and some HYVs more than others), and are likely to want to show their village performing well in this respect. Similarly the staff want to show the FLIA performing well. Thus, despite the staff's awareness of the unreliability of the figures, the register of land under each type of paddy variety is kept in elaborate and apparently meticulous detail - for this is a subject in which the government is keenly interested.

Finally, although the Agricultural Affairs staff are meant, according to their official list of duties, to provide links between the farmers and the other government agencies serving agriculture (notably the extension agents of the ORD and the credit officers of the NACF), in practice, according to SY staff, they do not do so. In practise, that is, they do not act as mediators or intermediaries between farmers and the other arms of government. Nor, relatedly, are there meetings for coordination and planning between FLIA staff and these other agencies.

Several staffers indicated that they disliked having to do the agricultural extension part of their job. The head of Agricultural Machinery, who had visited Taiwan, said Korea should adopt the Taiwanese arrangement, in which Irrigation Associations are concerned (as should be Korea's FLIAs) only with canal and pump operation and maintenance, and Farmers Associations are concerned with agricultural extension. He and others pointed to the existing confusion in agricultural extension arrangements in South Korea, where both the ORD and the NACF are responsible for agricultural extension in the same area; in FLIA areas, there is yet a third extension agency. A senior staffer related that SY had until four or five years ago separate sections for Agricultural Extension and Canal Operation. Then the Ministry of Agriculture ordered the Agricultural Extension Section to be closed, and he was glad, thinking this would allow more staff to be put on canal operation. But since then, the Ministry has put increasing pressure on the FLIAs to do more agricultural extension, creating a situation which he feels is confused and confusing. Part of the problem is that the staff do not feel well qualified in agricultural extension (and their in-service training is not intense, as we have noted). Another is that they see

canal operation as an entirely different kind of job to
agricultural extension; and one which because it entails
less direct involvement with farmers is both more
straightforward and more 'technical' (and perhaps of
higher prestige).

Still another element is what some staff described
as the growing frustrations of extension work in the
past two years or so, because farmers are no longer
putting their attention into rice growing; the farmers
now know how to get high yields and rather than try for
still higher yields, are giving their attention to non-
paddy agriculture (vegetables, livestock), or to non-
agricultural activities. But the FLIA's extension
service is specialised for irrigated agriculture, which
means for paddy. So the farmers, said my informants,
are no longer paying much attention to the FLIA staff.

A foreign irrigation engineer who visited nine FLIAs
in South Korea reported that he found this dislike of the
extension part of their jobs by Canal Operation and
Agricultural Extension staff to be general. [19]

Behind this dislike is probably a distaste for the
high pressure tactics which the government's high
priority to the attainment of HYV targets forces them,
as they see it, to adopt. It forces them to conflict
with farmers who don't want to take their advice.
Farmers' resistance has become worse since the mid 1970s
when several of the government's favoured varieties
have failed seriously, resulting in a loss of government
credibility. [20]

The government's response in the face of farmers'
reluctance has been to push even harder. Hence the
increasing pressure on the FLIA from the Ministry to do
more extension work. Having the FLIA as well as the ORD
and the NACF provide extension does mean that the density
of extension agents in the irrigated areas is
extraordinarily high. If we include only the agents of
the ORD and the FLIA (excluding those of the NACF, on
which I have no information), the average density is one
extension officer (excluding patrollers) to 243 farm
households and 208 hectares of cultivated land. [21]

MAINTENANCE

We have considered the functions of canal operation and
agricultural extension; now we consider more briefly the
maintenance function. [22]

In the spring, just before the canals are opened in
early April, the FLIA organises the maintenance of the
main and branch canals. The labour is provided by the
staff of the Maintenance section, in a supervisory
capacity, and by the patrollers and the farmers in a
labouring capacity. The patrollers and farmers are paid

the prevailing wage rate for agricultural labour, 3,200
won a day in 1979 (though according to one farmer, the
FLIA never pays the full amount, the rest being made up
with rice wine).   There is however no difficulty
getting enough labour because the farmers recognise some
obligation to help with the work, and turn the meal times
into festive occasions.   Normally each farmer works for
only a day or two, and only on the stretch of the canal
near his village.   The FLIA itself owns some heavy
earth-moving equipment for the desilting, and also hires
machinery from private contractors.
     The lower levels of the distribution and drainage
network are the responsibility of the farmers (farmers
say the FLIA is meant to be responsible for the
maintenance of all channels, but the farmers have to do
it because of the FLIA's default).   In the spring it
is customary for all the farmers with land bordering
a distribution channel to clean it of silt and refuse
together on the same day, each doing the bit that
borders his land (rather than working collectively).
The day is decided informally by the farmers under the
channel; a number of them may meet in the fields or in
the village and decide that the next day would be a good
time to do it, and then spread the word to the others.
Because of the small size of holdings, this work takes
each farmer no more than a few hours.   If a farmer
fails to do the work within a reasonable time and the
conveyance of the channel is likely to be impaired,
a variety of informal pressures will be placed upon him.
The equality of landholding and affluence in the villages
makes for an equality in confidence to speak up against
backsliders, and someone who fails to maintain his portion
of the ditch will be asked frequently and directly, by
many, to do so, and the case may be brought up at the
ban (sub-village) or village meeting (see below).   The
drainage channels are maintained in the same way, but with
much less care and diligence.
     After the spring maintenance the arrangements for
cleaning the lateral channels remain the same except that
the work is not done in unison: each farmer is expected
to do 'his' portion of the channel as the need arises. [23]
Subsequent maintenance on the main and branch canals is
done by the FLIA staff, though if a weed infestation
becomes particularly bad, for example, or there is a
flood, nearby farmers will be asked and will generally
agree to help cut the weeds or repair the damage without
pay.
     In general the standard of maintenance seems,
impressionistically, to be good on the farmers' channels,
and in many places less good in the main and branch
canals. The drainage channels at all levels are generally
full of weeds. One reason why the FLIA managers want
concrete lining is to cut down weed growth (especially

zizania latifolia, a tall rush-like plant). The weeds
not only slow water flow, but also provide breeding
grounds for pests and diseases.

As for the concrete structures, we have noted that
many gates are broken (in one Section , about 30 out of
90 gates). Just why is not clear, especially since many
of them are no more than fifteen years old. The harsh
winters (with temperatures well below freezing point)
may be part of the explanation. Vandalisation is
probably not.

TRAINING

Although there are no formal educational qualifications for recruitment to grade five, it is difficult to
pass the entry examination without a high school
background. Nowadays many new recruits have a diploma
from a post-high school technical college, after a two
year course.

Until 1978 in-service training for FLIA staff was
arranged by the provincial office which oversees all
FLIAs in the province, and on average an SY staff
member (grade 5, 4, 3 only) went on a two-week course
once every six years or so. (The ORD staff receive much
more intensive in-service training, with one to three
day courses several times a year, and one to two week
courses once every one to two years.) In 1978 the
Agricultural Development Corporation arranged a series
of courses for FLIA staff at its training centre near
Seoul, as the first year of what is planned to be a
permanent arrangement. Four times a year, some one
hundred to one hundred and fifty FLIA staff from across
the whole country will come to the training centre.
They will divide into four courses: machinery and
electricity; agricultural affairs, agricultural
engineering (land development); and administration
(the latter for two weeks, the others for three).
As before, the course will be open only to grades 5, 4
and 3 (not, in particular, to permanent employees, who
will continue to get virtually no in-service training).

The three week course in 'agricultural affairs'
has four subjects: operation and management of
irrigation water; pests and diseases; general
agriculture; increasing rice production. The subject of
'operation and management of irrigation water' is concerned
with activities below the outlet, not with main system
operation. The absence of any training in canal
operation helps to explain why the SY staff had
difficulty even in talking about the techniques of
rotational delivery: discussion of such techniques is
unfamiliar, and even the relevant words are unfamiliar,
being derived from Chinese (as is much of the more
technical vocabulary of irrigation).

CONCLUSION

SY canal system is characterised by an imbalance
between water control capacity and control utilisation.
The control capacity is relatively high, as set by the
density of gates, checks, measuring devices, and by the
effectiveness of communications facilities, such as radio,
telephone, motorcycles. With these physical facilities
it is possible to provide specified and varied quantities
of water down to low levels of the system. Control
capacity utilisation however is low. The high
estimated number of broken gates provides one
indication - as does the fact that precise information
is not available, even at Field Station level, on the
number of broken gates. More generally, we have noted
the absence of a wide range of data on basic physical
characteristics of the system and the environment, and
of recurrent information relevant to crop water demands.
We have noted also the absence of a plan for water
allocation, based upon specific identification of the
water used for the various stages of crop growth, which
stipulates how allocation is to be changed as the scarcity
of water changes.

The activities of the Field Stations and of the
Management bureau at HQ are, in fact, oriented towards
maintaining the physical security of the structures:
with spotting places in need of maintenance; helping
the patrollers arrange the maintenance, if small scale;
planning larger-scale maintenance; and raising and
lowering water-gates, cross-regulators, drainage gates,
etc. so as both to supply the whole command area and not
endanger the security of the structures by allowing the
water level at any point to rise too high. What they do
not do is to ration water, following rules or using
their judgement of water requirements and supply
possibilities.

In practice the system is run on a quasi-demand
rule, most of the time. As water becomes short in
relation to normal, there is some tightening up - at
Field Station level, the staff spend more of their time
on patrol along the canals, the gauges are read more
frequently, and, at HQ, more attention is given to the
question of how much water to release from the reservoirs.
The latter is the main means of rationing water. Not
even when total water supply (rainfall plus canal) fell
as far short of normal as it did in 1978 (well over 50
percent short) was rotational delivery attempted. The
other main response to water shortage is to use other
water sources, especially groundwater, which is not
normally used for reasons of expense and its depressing
effect on yields. (Similar failure to tap abundant
groundwater bodies for paddy irrigation is reported from
Japan .) [24] Obtaining water from groundwater and other

sources necessitates a very large increase in staff activity within the command area; but not an improvement in main system water delivery procedures.

In the longer term, too, the problem of increasing normal supplies is being tackled as a strictly technical problem: lining the canals, putting in more pump stations. (The fact that most of the pump stations have been built since 1965, and serve areas which could be fed by gravity-flow alone, supports the argument that they are being used as a substitute for improving water supply through the canals by tighter management.) These alternatives are of course expensive compared to management improvement; but much of the extra cost is borne by the farmers, who have no collective way of expressing their views.

Compare now the following account of the response to water shortage in the Yun Lin Irrigation Association in Taiwan. The Association has an irrigated area of approximately 67,000 hectares.

In "normal" periods water use efficiency can be estimated to vary between 50 and 60 percent. Gates are adjusted periodically, on the basis of the planned deliveries and using the measuring devices in an approximate mode. Allocations to different parts of the system are made with consideration of traditional water rights.... Water shortages up to 25-30 percent of normal flow are met by increasing the utilisation of local level control capability. Water is delivered with more precision relative to amount and timing, and adjustments reflecting specific needs, as determined by field observation, are made by agreements among the farmers and system personnel at the working station level. Water use efficiency increases to 75 or 80 percent. Yield generally is not adversely affected.

Water shortages in excess of 25 to 30 percent result in a shift to allocation of water on the basis of actual need (estimates again supported by field observations); traditional rights are no longer adhered to; measurement and control are increasingly precise, both with respect to rate and amount. Measuring devices are read more carefully and more frequently. The rate of flow is reduced, though the rotation interval between irrigations is not changed....Water use efficiency rises up to 90 percent or more.

Under conditions of extreme shortage, exemplified
by conditions in 1977 during which water supplies
dropped to 50 percent or less of normal, water
deliveries are timed to minutes; measuring
devices are calibrated frequently; irrigation
attendants monitor important control structures
on a twenty-four hour basis...., evapotranspiration and percolation are reduced through
the extension of the rotational interval;
special meetings are held with the irrigation
small groups to inform them of the water supply
situation and to encourage control practices
on the farms. Essentially 100 percent water
use efficiency is achieved, though it can be
anticipated that some yield reduction will
occur   (Levine, 1979, p. 4,5).

The organisational complexity of arrangements
for handling varying degrees of water scarcity in
the Yun Lin Irrigation Association mirrors the
greater complexity of irrigation organisation in
Taiwan generally, compared to South Korea. Again,
compare the following description with what we have
seen for South Korea:

...in Taiwan, when government policy emphasised
water use efficiency, but also stressed
productivity, equity and payment of irrigation
costs by the farmer beneficiaries, a series of
interacting efforts was conducted to implement
the policies.... The irrigation system operating
mechanisms included regular meetings between
system personnel and farmers to explain broad
policies, specific policies relative to water
delivery and operational procedures, election
by the farmers of an honorary group leader to
act as the intermediary between small groups
of farmers and the irrigation system (on a
continuing and operational basis);
performance rating of all system personnel;
a programme of field performance data collection,
and a number of others   (Levine, 1977a, p.46).

Why the striking difference with South Korea?
In both countries agricultural land is severely limited,
and has been for many decades. But in Taiwan the
opportunity cost of water is much higher: because of
climate and the prevalence of storage facilities, water
saved in one season can be used in the subsequent season;
in South Korea only one irrigated crop can be grown a
year, and during the irrigation season the amount of
irrigation required to supplement rainfall is, on average,
relatively small (though the economic value of that small

average supplement is high).   Therefore concern for
water use efficiency has been less in South Korea than
in Taiwan, where rotational irrigation was widely
introduced, with strong government promotion, after the
islandwide drought of 1954-55, and has become a normal
feature since then.
        Nevertheless, while the differing opportunity cost
of irrigation water may account for a large part of the
difference in organisational complexity, it would seem
likely that other factors deriving not from the physical
environment but from wider differences in social
organisation and policies are also important influences.
Just what these differences might be has to be left for
future research.   It may perhaps turn out that, contrary
to the impression given in most of the literature on
Taiwanese irrigation, the large Taiwanese capability to
respond to water shortage by increasing managerial control
over irrigation water is not economically 'efficient',
in the sense that the capability to respond to drought
is now so high that the expense of carrying this extra
capability (in terms of staff, equipment, physical
structures) in more normal times exceeds the gains from
having such a high level of capacity rather than a
lower one. 25   At least the question of the economic
costs and gains from a given level of drought protection
capacity must be raised.   If the Taiwanese government
has exceeded what might be economically justifiable
(by market criteria) one might look to the government's
perception of its dependence on rural support, its need
to be seen to be ensuring security of livelihood to the
nation's farmers, and this may perhaps provide a point
of contrast with South Korea.   But these are
speculations, to prompt further research.
        We have seen in this chapter how loosely defined
are the procedures which relate to SY FLIA's services
to farmers; we shall see in Chapter 6 how their
looseness of definition contrasts with the explicitness,
codification, elaborateness of procedures which relate
to income and spending, or to relations and mutual
responsibilities within the FLIA and between FLIA and
central government.   This asymmetry seems to go beyond
the fact that it is easier to codify the latter than the
former, and beyond the fact that codification of canal
operation is less necessary than in Taiwan, for example,
because of the different value of water.   The asymmetry
also reflects the point that rural state officials in
South Korea tend to be predominantly concerned with abiding
by or appearing to abide by procedures laid down from
above and achieving or appearing to achieve targets
decided from above, than with responding to what they
see to be the needs of farmers.   They are able to
maintain the asymmetry partly because farmers are
rigorously excluded from influence in their activities.

NOTES

1. Land development must, however, be an
important part of the whole picture, though a declining
part now that the rate of land development has slowed
down. It is nearly as big in terms of employees as
the bureau which handles system O & M and agricultural
extension, and is bigger in terms of expenditure. One
would expect that the need of land development staff
to find other essential tasks for them to do once the
land development work finishes would be strong. One
would expect also that farmers' sense of the justice
of their payments to the association must be affected by
their subjective comparison of benefits before and after
land development. However I treated land development
as peripheral to the central theme of how the irrigation
system is operated, and have little information on it.

2. However there are many siphons to allow for
cross-drainage.

3. Curiously, the province which occupies one
small corner of SY's area has not built a sufficiently
high flood embankment there, though the province with
the bank both upstream and downstream has done so.
The result is that every three or four years or so this
spot gets flooded. One wonders what lies behind this
failure - reasons to do with the natural environment,
different budget priorities between provinces, inter-
provincial rivalry, or 'frictions' between the FLIA and
the provincial administration.

4. Levine, 1979.

5. Wade, forthcoming.

6. On 'common irrigators', see Wade 1979, Levine
1976, Coward 1976. Reed, who studied two villages near
SY's area, both irrigated (though whether from a system
under SY's jurisdiction is not clear), reports, 'Unwritten
rules cover water use at the village level. Farmers
must coordinate their use of water in such a way that all
other farmers receive their share....Conflict at the
village level over water doesn't seem to be a serious
problem, but a more serious issue is conflict with the
Irrigation Cooperative (presumably the FLIA) over water
flow decisions and with other villages over water
"theft"' (1979, p. 110). Interestingly, having said
that conflict over water use at village level is not a
serious problem, Reed goes on to say that in (at least)
one of the two villages water is often scarce, because
it is located at the tail end of the canal. Reed does
not say why and how this scarcity does not give rise to
serious conflict. He relates that village representatives were sent to the Irrigation Cooperative to complain
about water shortage; but does not say what happened
(1979, p. 110).

7. Personal communication.

8. Eyre (1955), writing about a Japanese irrigation system in the early 1950s, reported a similar lack of attention to flow measurements. The system had an irrigated area of 4,000 hectares of paddy. 'Among the many problems in regularising the Takahashi River flow and distributing it equitably is the lack of detailed statistics on the seasonal volume. Present irrigation arrangements, based on upstream rights and historical precedents, make more accurate and detailed data of flow characteristics unessential. Also, prefectural and national agencies working in the field of water resources, which normally could be regarded as interested in river development and use, have given flow measurement scant attention' (216). Again, 'As with the river flow, little attention has been given to measurement of the volume of water drawn off into the system. It is known that the intake pipe permits the entry of a maximum seven tons of water a second, but the frequency of the maximum, the volume of average flow, and the degree of seasonal fluctuation have never been ascertained. Water supplies are either enough or not enough. If enough, operations continue serenely, but shortages are soon revealed by the farmers' protests... ' (203).

9. Given the forestation coefficient, the conveyance losses coefficient, a percolation rate, and the ratio of the catchment area to the benefited area, the Irrigation Requirement can be calculated (the depth of irrigation water per hectare needed to sustain the crop in the worst drought likely in ten years). The Irrigation Requirement multiplied by the benefited area gives the 'required storage', which can be compared against actual storage. Using a forestation coefficient of 1, a losses coefficient of 20 percent, a percolation rate of 3 mm/day, one of the four main reservoirs has an actual storage greater than required, the other three fail by not more than ten percent to meet required storage. But the conclusions are highly sensitive to the values of the parameters, and these are quite uncertain. SY staff had never made calculations of this sort, and even staff at the Agricultural Development Corporation's head office were unclear about what plausible values were. The losses coefficient in particular seems much too low; to the extent that it is too low the actual storage capacity would fail by a bigger margin to meet the required capacity, other things being equal.

10. The averages from the nearest state meterological station, 30 kilometres to the north on the same coastal plain, are 72 mm and 82 mm for April and May.

11. FLIA records show the following average yields of rice per 0.1 hectares: 1974 - 410; 1975 - 400; 1976 - 430 (another table gives 457); 1977 - 504; 1978 - 431.

12. I suspect this figure is too low; a figure of roughly twice this area seems, impressionistically, more likely.

13. Compare Kim's account of the nation-wide measures to fight the 1976 drought: 'noteworthy was the fact that the 1976 drought strikes have motivated not only the people in the agricultural sector but those in business and other non-agricultural occupations to stand up in line to fight together against the ill-effects of the natural disaster' (1978, p. 69).

14. Levine, 1979, Maass & Anderson, 1978.

15. Levine et al. 1976, Wen 1977.

16. Experimental results in South Korea have shown paddy yields in plots irrigated intermittently (once in eight days) to be 27 percent higher on average than continuously irrigated test plots, with a water saving of 52 percent (Ryu 1972, p. 337).

17. The SY FLIA prints a list of duties for each Section office, based on a model list prepared by the Ministry of Agriculture. Under Agricultural Affairs section are listed 29 duties: 1. Irrigation. 2. Weather forecasting and measuring. 3. Plan against flood and drought. 4. Investigate crop damage and calculate water charge reduction. 5. Measure water in reservoir and flow in canals. 6. Plant trees around reservoir and protect trees. 7. Control water gate of reservoirs. 8. Keep information on agricultural tools and machinery to make available to farmers. 9. O & M of agricultural tools. 10. Compile statistics on agricultural affairs. 11. Prepare plan for increasing rice production. 12. Investigate water requirements. 13. Survey irrigated area. 14. Prepare contracts for the supply of water outside the command area. 15. ? 16. Supervise patrollers. 17. Encourage Hueng Nong Gye (farmers' associations). 18. Increase soil fertility and double cropping. 19. Increase non-chemical fertiliser production. 20. Manage agricultural machinery project. 21. Compensate farmers across whose land emergency supply ditches dug. 22. Help farmers making application (to other branches of government) in connection with agricultural affairs. 23. General office administration. 24. Increase yield in agriculture by improved farming methods. 25. Make experimental rice paddies and demonstration plots. 26. Spread improved seed varieties. 27. Help farmers to protect plants against pests and diseases. 28. Raise fish in reservoirs. 29. Raise farmers' incomes by promoting products in addition to rice, and give farmers' Saemaul Movement guidance.

18. Steinberg et al, 1980
19. Personal communication.
20. See Reed, 1979, p. 224.
21. The Rural Guidance Office (the ORD office at county level) has 47 extension staff for 19,500 households and 20,500 hectares of paddy and upland crops, in the county which occupies the largest part of SY' s area amongst the five counties. Assuming this density to apply over the whole, the figures in the text are arrived at by combination with the average for the FLIA, 30 extension staff for 16,750 households and 11,500 hectares of paddy.
22. The formal list of duties for the Maintenance Section includes: 1. Maintenance of all facilities. 2. Investigation and design of all facilities. 3. Help supervise construction of new facilities. 4. Make maintenance budgets. 5. Make statistics about irrigation facilities. 6. Recovery and repayment for damages caused to facilities. 7. Management and operation, maintenance and repair of pump stations. 8. Buying and lending facilities. 9. ? 10. Prepare plan against drought, flood, wind disasters. 11. Survey irrigated area. 12. Build new ditches during emergencies. 13. Keep records of all facilities. 14. ? 15. Arrange for materials to be ready for construction projects. 16. Investigation of government-owned land to use for irrigation. 17. O & M of tractors, cranes and other tracked vehicles. 18. Help farmers change use of land from paddy to other, with prior permission. 19. O & M of telephone and radio systems. 20. Arranging tools and equipment for construction projects, owned or hired. 21. Paying rental fee for vehicles and tools. 22. Maintaining survey equipment.
23. Reed, in his study of two irrigated villages near SY's area, reports, 'At the village level maintenance of irrigation channels is not a serious problem. Each spring teams are formed to remove accumulated silt and repair eroded banks along the major channels in the village, while individual farmers are responsible for the ditches supplying their own fields. Otherwise joint action is necessary only in times of emergency - if there is a break in a canal bank, for example' (1979, p. 110).
24. Eyre 1955,p.198 'Although most of the surface water supply is at least partly utilised, abundant groundwater bodies known to exist in many of the alluvial low-lands have hardly been tapped. Little more than one percent of the irrigation water is drawn from wells, and they are usually pressed into service only in paddies adjacent to stream beds or are used as supplementary sources in times of drought'.
25. A point suggested to me by Gilbert Levine.

5
The Farmers and the System

Across South and Southeast Asia, the formation of irrigator groups is a standard component of policies to improve irrigation, on the assumption that the organisation of farmers into such groups will result in improved water management at field level. The irrigator groups are to be the means of achieving one prerequisite for sound management of an irrigation system: a set of procedures for keeping the managers continuously informed about the farmers' situations and for making judgements about what share of the available supply farmers in different localities should be given. Irrigator groups are also to be the means of organising the maintenance of conveyance and drainage channels below the outlet. With this institutional channel for farmer-system communication, it is expected that the system will become more responsive to the farmers' needs and preferences, that the farmers will be better informed about water policies and operational aspects, and consequently will become more confident of receiving a reliable supply. With increased confidence, farmers will be less likely to waste water in order to be sure of getting enough, and more likely to maintain structures below the outlet; water use efficiency[1] will therefore increase. Farmers' propensity to invest in higher levels of inputs will also increase.

Effective liaison between canal staff and irrigators is an often noted characteristic of Taiwan's Irrigation Associations. The key institution is the Irrigation Small Group, comprising about 100 farmers, and the elected honorary group leader. Directly, and indirectly through the leader, the farmers interact with Working Station personnel to provide the basic link in the communication channel. Farmer needs and complaints of a minor nature are settled at this level. Small Group meetings with Working Station staff are held three or four times per crop season.[2]

South Korea's Hueng Nong Gye (literally, Cooperative Groups for the Promotion of Agriculture, HNG hereafter)

are often likened to Taiwan's Small Groups. In official
and semi-official publications on South Korean irrigation organisation, they are ascribed with a similar
role in the overall organisation of land and water use
projects. Thus the World Bank: 'Land Improvement
Associations organise members into "Hungnonge" (sic)
groups, a form of farmers' clubs for promoting technical
improvement of irrigated farming' (World Bank, 1973,
Annex 6, p.16). Official irrigation statistics reg-
ularly include a column for 'number of Hueng Nong Gye'
in each FLIA, county, province, and the nation as a
whole.

One might anticipate from the previous chapter that
the reality is different. We shall see here that the
word 'club' quite inappropriately implies a tangible,
corporate existence for the HNG. It is not even the
case that the official publications represent the reality
as the government would like it to be and is striving to
create. The divorce between the official picture and
the reality on the ground is stable; no attempts are
being made to foster the effective functioning of the
HNG. It is enough that they appear in the statistics
and organisation charts.

THE REALITY OF THE HUENG NONG GYE

The smallest administrative unit in South Korea is
the ban, fourteen to twenty households which live
adjacently, grouped under the ban-jang, the ban headman.
During the period of the Park government (1961 to 1979)
these have become important units of social mobilisation
and control. Once a month, on the 25th day, all ban in
South Korea are to meet to discuss local and national
issues; sometimes the ban meetings join together in a
village meeting. Each household sends one representative.
In villages this representative is normally the male head
of the household, who is normally a farmer.[3] Unsurprisingly much of the discussion is about farming. This
gathering of ban or village,then, constitutes a kind of
farmers' association. However it differs from an association in that membership is not voluntary, and strong
social pressures are placed on households to attend.

The nearest corporate body to the HNG is the ban or
village meeting. When a HNG leader is asked when the
HNG meets, he will reply that it meets at the same time
and place as the ban or village meeting. There is in
effect one 'HNG' per village; the statistics on 'number
of HNGs' refer simply to the number of villages (ri)
watered from FLIA systems. The World Bank's statement
quoted earlier that 'Land Improvement Associations
organise members into "Hungnonge" groups, a form of
farmers' club for promoting technical improvement of

irrigated farming', is thus doubly misleading: not only do the HNG as such not exist on the ground, but the FLIA has no role in initiating or sustaining the nearest real equivalent - the ban and village meetings are supervised by the Ministry of Home Affairs and its sub-national agencies.

THE HUENG NONG GYE LEADER

However, the FLIA does require that there be one person in each village designated as HNG leader. The ban groups ask one of the wealthier and/or more articulate farmers in each village to undertake this responsibility. People do not like being HNG leader, for there is no reward, either material [4] or honorary, attached to the position, and the duties can be inconvenient. At the same time the person must be capable of dealing with the FLIA staff, for it is through him that much of the communication between FLIA and farmers comes. He and the patroller are the critical links in the communication chain. Hence pressure is put on men of relative wealth, age, experience and articulateness. If a village does not succeed in getting someone to take the job, the Field Station staff will appoint someone - authority to appoint all HNG leaders lies with the head of the Station, but in practice the appointment is usually on the recommendation of the village chief.

What do the HNG leaders do? Significantly, the FLIA has no list of duties and responsibilities of HNG leaders - in contrast to the detailed codification of such matters for FLIA staff. One defined his function as follows: First, to see that field channels below the outlet are kept adequately maintained (and speak to farmers who are falling behind), and to see that when the main canal (and drainage channel) near his village are being cleaned at the start of the season, enough men from his village go to help. Second, to help spot and fight plant pests and diseases. Third, to get farmers in his village to pay their water charges promptly. Fourth, to contact the patroller about local water problems, and persuade 'members' not to waste water. (Water delivery problems were last on his list.) He did not mention two other important functions: to help the village chief select the patroller, if the patroller is to come from his village (that is, if the village is the most central in the jurisdiction to be covered by the patroller); and to pass on statistics of area under different paddy varieties, area ploughed (by ten-day intervals), area harvested, and other information requested by the FLIA. In short, the HNG leader is primarily the FLIA's agent in each village, as well as one of the farmers' two main channels of access to the FLIA.

The HNG leaders in each Field Station are called together twice a year to meet with the Field Station staff
at the Field Station, where they are told about disease
and pest control measures and may discuss problems of
water distribution and maintenance. They then have
lunch together, paid for by the FLIA. This is the extent of formal meetings and training for the HNG leaders.
   The patrollers, as we have seen, have more frequent
interaction with the FLIA staff, and receive more frequent
instructions on matters such as spotting pests and diseases. At the same time they are 'locals',
permanent residents of the area which they guard. On
the other hand, they are normally of relatively low
status within the village, unlike the HNG leader.

FARMERS' ACCESS

   The farmers' access to the FLIA, then, is mediated
by these two roles. One rarely sees a farmer at a
Field Station office - and virtually never at the HQ
building. According to both staff and farmers, it is
almost unknown for farmers to write letters to the FLIA
suggesting improvements or raising complaints. My
question as to whether the (elected) National Assembly
members could be used as a means of access was greeted
by a 'don't-be-so-silly' laugh: National Assembly
members don't interest themselves in such things.
   One farmer who had written several times to the FLIA
suggesting improvements for his area was a retired
banker, who, very unusually, had decided to 'go back to
the land' on his retirement (and attracted national press
praise for his decision). He bought a relatively large
holding (2.5 hectares) in the area of SY FLIA. He was
concerned, he said, at how reluctant the farmers were
to take up issues with the FLIA, and how reluctant the
FLIA was to listen to what they had to say. If he had
not been highly educated, he said, the staff would not
have responded to his suggestions - not even for such
elementary things as railings along the walk-way out to
the outlet pipe in the reservoir, despite the danger the
absence of such railings posed for children. And, he
added sadly, if he hadn't written to the FLIA about the
railings, none of his neighbours would have. He had
heard of no-one else who had written to the FLIA to make
a suggestion.
   Why not? Because the farmers don't trust the FLIA's
answers, he said, and have no information with which to
challenge what the FLIA tells them. In any case, the
FLIA has no power, but has only to do what the Ministry
of Agriculture tells it. What were the possibilities of
giving the farmers more access to the FLIA, or even some
influence in its decisions? One has to understand, he

said, the 'special security problem of Korea' as the
reason why this could not be done, why the government
had to keep tight control, and why insufficient funds
were available to modernise the systems (due to the
overriding demands of the defence budget).

Another farmer, of more typical background but
also with a relatively large holding, thought it wrong
that the Ministry of Agriculture rather than the farmers
appointed the President. He went on to say that the
farmers regard the staff of the FLIA as 'just tax
collectors'. Having made such a strong criticism, he
then softened the impression as he explained how the
present situation arose. Like the first man, he invoked the special security problem of Korea as the
reason why the farmers had no influence, and by the end
of his elaboration on this theme was almost saying, in
contrast to his first reaction, that it was necessary
that the farmers had no influence. The 'tax collector'
image of the FLIA staff is widely shared, and is implied
by the very word farmers use for payments to the FLIA:
whereas the FLIA staff refer to these payments as bi,
which means a 'cost', a 'fare', a 'due', the farmers say
se(i), which means 'tax' - the officials' word suggests
a contract (if you don't want the water you don't pay),
the farmers' implies no choice and a coercive sanction.

There is one means by which the farmers are apparently
at least kept informed about the FLIA's policies and personnel: the 'SY Public Newspaper', published four times
a year, and distributed free to all farmers in the
irrigated area. Its first issue was in 1975; before
then, nothing. Eash issue has a statement from the
President (with his photo) and another from the Manager
(with his photo), drawing attention to current farming
problems. Other articles may be about the need for
farmers to make more non-chemical fertiliser, the
advantages of machine transplanting; at the end of the
financial year the FLIA's past and planned budget is
reproduced. Several points about the contents are worth
noting: none of the articles refer to the specific
situations of SY farmers or the SY area; there has been
almost nothing about the SY staff, or about SY policy
options, or SY water plans and operational procedures;
no articles or letters by farmers ever appear; the
photos show the staff, and the FLIA's equipment and
buildings, but farmers are shown only when posing in
training meetings with staff; and finally, the articles
are written using many Chinese characters which are
familiar only to the relatively highly educated.

The paper is the responsibility of a young 'permanent employee' on the administrative side. He writes the
President's and Manager's statements, and often they do
not even see the statements before publication. His

qualifications for writing the Manager's statement on the
theme of, say, 'Save irrigation water even when it is
sufficient', are nil, and this is reflected in the
quality of the statements? The rest of the paper (other
than the budget statements) is made up of articles which
he takes (unacknowledged) from the pages of the provincial
newspaper, whose printer also prints the SY newspaper.
Nobody in the FLIA other than he takes any interest in
the paper. The Ministry of Agriculture obliges them to
print it.

It should be noted that SY's farmers are relatively
highly educated and exposed to urban influences (because
of the area's proximity to Seoul and its location on a
main transport route). Their exclusion is not because
they lack the capacity for expression that education
tends to confer.

ACCOUNTABILITY: WATER CHARGE COLLECTION

It might be thought that the dependence of the FLIA
for its income (including salary and wages of staff) on
farmers' payment of water charges would give the farmers
some means of making the staff accountable to them. If
dissatisfied with the service, they could withhold payment of charges until their complaints were considered
and the service improved. One would expect any organisation whose staff depend on payments from clients for
their wages and salares, but which is not in a position
to withhold its service from a client who does not pay,
to give careful attention to the question of how to
avoid non-payment. It is said that in Taiwan's Irrigation Associations the link between water charges and
budget does indeed operate as a means of keeping the
staff accountable.[6] In South Korea, however, the link
is largely broken through the construction of powerful
incentives for prompt payment regardless of water
service, backed by strong coercive sanctions against
defaulters.

The staff of SY FLIA put a great deal of effort into
ensuring that the farmers pay their water charges.
Administering the collection arrangements and making the
assessments, is, impressionistically (there is no quantitative evidence), a major use of the staff's labour time.

The main technique is the competition. Substantial
monetary prizes are given to the villages (described as
'to the HNGs') whose farmers all pay their assessed
charges earlier rather than later. Most of the twelve
small irrigation districts have their own competition-
and the four-reservoir system is divided into sub-
districts, each with its own. (The largest Field
Station, with an area of 4,000 hectares, has six competitions.) In this way the number of villages competing

against each other is kept small (ten to twenty), the intensity of the incentive correspondingly high. The value of the prize money depends on the total charges to be collected from the district. A smaller than average amount of prize money is 170,000 won, divided into 50,000 won for first prize, two second prizes of 30,000, and three third prizes of 20,000 won. The money is used towards a village project (a bridge or access road, for example), it is said. Altogether 4,400,000 won was spent on prize money for HNG water charge collection competitions in 1978, equal to half of one percent of the total money collected through water charges. In addition to the HNG competitions, the Field Stations also compete amongst themselves to be first with all charges paid up. In 1978 400,000 won went in Working Station prize money for this purpose. The money is usually used for a feast, often with some of the HNG leaders from the Working Station's area as well as the staff taking part.

In this way the collective (village) incentives for individual compliance are made strong (stronger than in Taiwan, because of the larger prize money and the smaller number of competitors in each separate competition).[7]

However, if an individual has still not paid thirty days after receiving the assessment notice, he is sent a letter informing him that as long as he pays within another fifteen days he will only have to pay an extra 10 percent penalty. (There are ill-defined rights of appeal, with final appeal to the President of the FLIA, but no attempt is made to remind farmers of this right.) If payment is not received by the end of the fifteen days the police are sent to sequester goods valued at the amount of arrears. The goods are held for another fifteen days before being sold if payment has still not been received. In SY FLIA there have been no cases of goods being sold, say its officials.

Hence one can understand why the level of water charge payment is always in excess of 99 percent of assessments, and why the dependence of staff income on water charge payment by farmers is not a means of disciplining the staff to operate the system effectively. Compare some propositions commonly adduced to explain effective system operation in Taiwan: that (in Abel's words),

If collections are poor, revenue will not be adequate to cover operating costs and will eventually result in a reduction in the size of the association's staff ... The willingness of farmers to pay their fees depends heavily on how well the irrigation associations are operated, i.e., the amount and timeliness

of water received. The better the system is managed,
the more willing the farmers will be to pay their
fees.... Thus, job security and levels of remuner-
ation for management personnel are tied directly to
how well a system is managed (1975, p.24).

My hypothesis is that the difference with South
Korea is due to incentives and coercive sanctions which
are in South Korea so much higher for prompt payment of
charges that the link between system operation and
farmers' payment is largely broken.

OTHER COMPETITIONS

In addition to the water charge collection, the FLIA
organises other competitions both for farmers and for
Field Stations. The goals and the form and value of the
prizes vary from year to year depending on what objectives the FLIA (and Ministry of Agriculture) wishes to
emphasise. Normally however there are farmers' competitions for rice yields, barley yields (now dropped since
the Ministry of Agriculture has given up trying to
promote barley in this part of South Korea), and production of non-chemical fertiliser. Sometime's the prizes
are in money, sometimes in objects like watches or
clocks.[8] There is normally a competition for Field
Stations in production of non-chemical fertiliser (on
the assumption of a demonstration effect - if farmers
see the staff diligently making compost beside the
Station office they too will be encouraged to do so);
and sometimes for canal maintenance, or water distribution, or pest and disease control. In the latter two
cases, the competition is ex post - prizes will be
awarded for good performance in the face of a pest
attack or water shortage, without a competition having
been declared in advance. Between Field Stations the
prizes are mainly non-material, in the form of certificates awarded by the President of the FLIA; but may
include a pen or other small token for the head of the
Station. In one recent year there was an award to the
'model patroller', but this has not been continued (for
reasons which are not clear). All competitions and
awards are organised centrally at HQ, even those wholly
within a particular Section.

ACCOUNTABILITY: NEW COMMUNITY MOVEMENT

Since 1975 FLIA staff have been directed to give
more attention to serving farmers, under the aegis of
the New Community (Saemaul) Movement. This began as a
community development programme in the early 1970s,
based avowedly on the principles of 'diligence, self-

reliance, cooperation'. Subsequently, President Park declared it 'a national spiritual revolution for a better way of life', 'a driving force for nation build-ing' via increased productivity, community participation in local projects, and education in the policies of the present government and its leader. Its scope has been extended to urban areas, private firms, government departments, and an elaborate bureaucracy has been established to administer its activities, with offices at each level of government culminating in an important office within the Blue House (President Park's own administration). All success is attributed to President Park.[9]

We shall consider later in more detail what the FLIA staff have to do in pursuing New Community instructions. Here the point to note is that one part of the long New Community Movement questionnaire which the FLIA has to answer quarterly is titled 'Devotion to the service of farmers'. Under this section the FLIA has to report what it is doing and planning to do to further this devotion. In the returns for 1979 a number of projects were mentioned:

1. Patrollers are to watch their language with farmers at transplanting time, when farmers tend to be tense.
2. Staff from HQ will go to Field Station offices once a month in order to give farmers better access to them.
3. On that day of the month, the HQ and the Field Stations will be open to farmers to come and discuss their problems with staff, from 13:00 to 18:00 hours. Outside experts may also be invited to attend.
4. More discussions should be held with HNGs (sic) about water charges.
5. The farmers are to be encouraged to telephone, send a letter or card, or use a Suggestions Box, in order to report staff misbehaviour or suggest changes. The farmers are to be encouraged to telephone the FLIA's President himself if they wish to.

These plans were communicated upwards through the New Community Movement hierarchy; none, however, appeared in the SY Public Newspaper. A Suggestions Box was indeed installed - in the HQ building hidden behind a screen in the main entrance (alongside another box, labelled 'Let's Give To The Poor'). No Station offices had installed a Suggestions Box by mid 1979.

OTHER MEANS OF ACCOUNTABILITY

To leave the discussion of farmers' access and staff accountability at this point would be misleading. Because of the density of staff, the routines of the patrollers and the arrangements for supervision of patrollers, and also because of the absence of a status gulf between staff and farmers (such as one tends to find in South Asia), there is frequent interaction between staff and farmers - but on a person-to-person rather than a group basis. (However, it is not the general case that this interaction is facilitated by common social origins and residence; some but not a majority of the staff are sons or brothers of farmers, but most of these now live in the towns and spend most of their leisure time with townspeople.)

Through this personal interaction, as well as via the HNG leaders, farmers' complaints, if felt by many, do get through to the staff. The most potent and potentially divisive issue, as one might expect, is water charges (and not only at SY FLIA: in a recent survey of 360 FLIA farmers throughout the country, over 80 percent said they thought water charges are too high).[10] The SY staff's normal response is, in the words of the head of Agricultural Affairs, 'If water charge increases are reasonable, the farmers have no lawful reaction'. In practice, however, the staff are very sensitive (at least in 1979) to the farmers' unwillingness to pay yet higher charges. In 1977 the charges were increased substantially (by about 35 percent on the previous year's average), and many farmers complained. The FLIA's response was to call the HNG leaders to special meetings at the Field Stations to explain to them why higher charges were necessary (illustrating the FLIA's use of HNG leaders as their agents in the villages). The staff's hostile reaction to a proposed national reform in FLIA operation (which we consider later) was based in large part on the fear that water charges would have to go up again if the reform were implemented - though they themselves stood to get substantial income increases.

In addition to making use of the many occasions for person-to-person contact with staff, farmers also can influence their own water service through influence on the choice of the patroller for their area. Formally the appointment of patrollers is in the hands of the Field Station heads, but in practice they rely on nominations from the village chief and HNG leader of the central village in each jurisdiction. The village chief and HNG leader in turn are likely to sound out opinion more widely. It happens not infrequently that a patroller is not re-appointed because of indifferent performance the previous season, in the eyes of the local farmers.

WHY DO THE FARMERS NOT HAVE A BIGGER ROLE?

The reasons why the farmers do not have a bigger role in the FLIA do not include a lack of organisational capacity. Korean villages have had a long tradition of self-government. Most major decisions were taken informally by a small group of influential, generally wealthy men, and meetings open to all adult men were also held periodically at which anyone could speak his mind. The result was a form of consensual, participatory politics directed by a small elite.[11]

Through this organisation community work projects, such as the construction and repair of roads, dikes, bridges, were carried out. When a road or bridge needed repair, the village head would call a meeting of all family heads. Decisions were made as to when the work was to be done and how many days of labour each family was to provide. The labour was furnished without payment. When a household could not provide labour, it was expected to contribute cash, food, or drink. Since the contribution was meant to be voluntary, no explicit penalties could be levied on those not participating. But households which did not were subject to typically severe moral censure and social isolation[12] - the distinction in rural Korea between voluntary and corvee labour, donations and extortions, has never been sharp. This form of organisation is still used today for undertaking community work projects, though with much more government direction; and is used for mobilising farmers for the annual maintenance of irrigation canals by the FLIA.

Nowadays arrangements are more formalised through the establishment in each village (at government initiative) of a 'village development committee', which includes the village head, the New Community leader, the HNG leader, the ban chiefs, and other influentials. It meets often through the year to discuss issues; and there are also once or a few times yearly meetings of all household heads at which the overall development plans for the village have to be approved, 'usually after extended and lively discussion', according to one study (Brandt and Lee, 1977, p.40).

Further, within almost every Korean village are one or more mutual aid associations (gye), most frequently to assist members in paying for funerals and weddings (and also at the same time to foster friendship ties).[13] The gye are now, since the 1961 change of government, virtually the only private organisations in the villages; the other organisations are government sponsored and

usually government supervised.[14] The informal gathering
of young men, a long standing village tradition, also
continues today but under the wing of the central government, in the form of various centrally-directed
youth associations. And traditionally - still but to
a lesser extent today - there were many occasions during
the year when people joined together in group activities
of a ritual, economic, social, recreational nature,
expressing village reciprocity and interdependence with
little calculation of individual cost or profit.[15]

In short, Korean villagers have much experience of
deliberately concerting their actions in some collective
interest. Water users' associations could readily have
been operated in this context.

That the farmers have not been given any formal role
in the operation of the FLIA is due, in part, to conditions of water supply ; in particular, to the lack of
concern for high water use efficiency and water productivity. In Taiwan the responsibilities of the Irrigator
Small Groups came to be expanded and closely defined as
part of the general attempt to increase the water control capacity on irrigation systems, and thereby to
increase water efficiency and productivity.

However under any publicly-operated irrigation
system one would expect the structure of relations
between irrigators and irrigation staff to be shaped
not only (and in general not mainly) by response to
environmental conditions, but also by the structure of
government-populace relations more generally. Perhaps
where, as in Taiwan, concern for making the best use of
water is high, relations between irrigators and system
personnel are structured so as to give irrigators in
this specific context more influence than is normal in
government-populace relations in Taiwan, because of the
importance for sound management of a set of procedures
for keeping continuously informed about the irrigators'
situations and needs. Conversely, where concern for
water efficiency is not high, one might expect relations
between irrigators and system personnel to be relatively
more shaped by, less distinct from, the wider norms of
government-populace relations. In South Korea irrigator-
system relations mirror the wider structure of power.

We need to recall that for centuries Korea has been
a self-governing, highly centralised agrarian-bureaucratic
kingdom. Land tended to be in the hands of family proprietorships, with a close matching of cultivation and
ownership; and tended to be relatively equally distributed. Relatedly, local concentrations of power were
relatively weak vis-a-vis the central government in
Seoul.[16] The pattern of land holding (but not the
extent of centralisation) changed towards a landlord-
tenant structure during Korea's period as a Japanese

colony (1910-45); but was restored to one of owner-cultivators by the post-Second World War land reform. Since then land has remained concentrated in the hands of family owner-cultivators, most of whom own less than three hectares and employ little non-family labour. They produce their own subsistence, and are little connected with vertical food-processing and manufaturing chains.

In this structure there has been since the land reform no landlord group to exercise power, to maintain social stability and to supply the cities with food; nor to act as a focus of resistance to the government, a channel for the articulation of local grievances. There has therefore been an unusual opportunity, and an unusual need for the state to control a mass of small farmers directly. When little differentiation exists within the locality, there are likely to be no clear oppositions which could drive those who see themselves (and are seen by others) as more privileged to identify with the state's local agents. Hence there is a need for the state to undertake the task of control more directly. At the same time the opportunities for doing so are not limited by the need to share power with local landlords. Small-scale agriculture has been thoroughly embraced by the large-scale state.

Since 1961 there has been no popular participation in the highly centralised administration of rural areas. Administrative control of governmental affairs in rural areas is close, so close as to almost preclude anyone exercising a leadership role who is opposed to the present government.[17] The government has created several new leadership roles at village level, making these roles and the traditional role of village chief focal points of contact between government and populace, and taking a large hand in the appointment of incumbents. The village chief is appointed by the township chief (a full-time government official),'usually after consultation with influential local farmers' (Brandt and Lee 1977, p.4). The post is honorary, but the work heavy: he is responsible for collecting a large number of statistics, supervising tax collections, mobilising village labour for projects (mostly work on township roads); is required to attend the township office frequently to receive a steady stream of orders and agricultural guidance; is to promote loyalty to the regime and social harmony; and tries to represent the interests of his villagers to the authorities.[18] The New Community Movement leader is a second important role. In this case selection is formally with villagers, but township officials exert much influence and central government lays down the criteria to be used. (The fact that the post of HNG leader is not usually appointed by the FLIA may reflect the lack of importance

attached by government to irrigation organisation.)[19]
The village is the only level at which leaders are
chosen and decisions arrived at by popular participation.

While the economic growth of the 1960s and 1970s,
reinforced by the New Community Movement of the 1970s,
has tightened links between villagers and the bureaucracy, these take the form of bringing technology,
resources, advice, orders, controls in, and taking
agricultural products out.[20] But as one study observes,
'There is some flow of information from the villages
that is fed back into the administrative decision-making
process, but it is probably minimal' (Brandt and Lee,
1977, p.131). Another study of South Korean rural
administration comments in the same vein that, '"Participation" in rural development programs generally
means responding obediently (or at least giving the
impression of responding obediently) to government
programs' (Aqua, 1974, p.66). A United Nations report
on a watershed management project in South Korea stated
that, 'The tendency [of South Korean officials] to issue
instructions from offices instead of solving problems
through discussions and personal guidance in the field
caused some problems. The village is not just one or
two leaders to whom government officers can issue
instructions' (UNDP/FAO, 1974, p.256).

As these points suggest, relations between populace
and government take place within a markedly hierarchical,
authoritarian structure. A Korean scholar sums it up
as follows:

The attitude of administrators toward the clients is
governed by the hierarchical norm. Administrators
are supposed to rule and, at best, to teach and
guide the people. Governmental action is generally
regarded as a favor rather than as an obligation.
Consequently the clientele are in the position of
begging for special favors rather than requesting
the government's abidance with legal provisions.
At best, governmental favors are handed out because
of sympathy toward the people, and at worst, because
of paybacks by clients to particular administrators'
(Suk-choon Cho, 1975, p.75).

This account however oversimplifies the complexity of
the issue. The issue, from the government's point of
view, is how to persuade or make the farmers do what
the government wants. Orders formulated at the top can
come down the bureaucratic hierarchy fast until they
reach the lowest administrative office at the township
(myon). There is then a gap, which somehow has to be
crossed. Often the lowest level officials will themselves be under heavy pressure to meet specified

targets and can choose, so to speak, between coercion, persuasion, or falsification of the records in order to do so.

One component of the strategy for obtaining farmers' compliance, as we have seen, is appointment of incumbents to key village leadership positions, which are made the focal point of government-villager relations. Specifically, these leaders are given responsibility for the achievements of the village's targets (for example, on HYV area).

Their identification with government orders is not left to chance or local circumstances. They receive intensive political education, especially through the New Community Movement, to promote their loyalty (and indirectly that of those they influence) to the nation, President Park, the government, and the government's local agents. The populace is also reached more directly for political education not only through the commercial press (closely supervised by government) and television (now common in rural households near towns, and government controlled), but also through the ban meetings. Special newspapers are produced in each province for free distribution prior to the monthly ban meetings, which in addition to explaining national policies (like what the government is doing about the oil price rise), and giving agricultural instructions (on pests and diseases), have much space devoted to topics of nationalism and anti-communism/North Korea.[21]

A third important technique is the government-orchestrated competition. Big prizes are given for high yields (especially in paddy) at township, county, provincial, and national levels, culminating in highly prestigious awards from President Park himself. The same instrument is used in the New Community Movement.[22] Villages which used the initial allocation of cement well were given more cement plus steel rods the following year (1971), to promote a spirit of constructive competition in which less successful villages would strive to follow those that got more help. In 1973 a national New Community Movement convention was attended by some 4,000 people selected for their villages' superior achievements under the programme; in 1975, the national rally was attended by over 7,000, of whom 214 were singled out for special awards, and grants of extra government resources were awarded to 2,500 villages throughout the country which had done well in the previous period.

Villages have now been classified into three ranks: 'basic' or underdeveloped villages; 'self-helping' villages; and 'independent' villages. The criteria of classification are worth noting for their formal

similarity to the criteria which are proposed to be used
to rank the FLIAs, as part of the proposed FLIA reform,
to be discussed in Chapter 7:

		Type of Village	
	Basic	Self-helping	Independent
% of rice fields which are irrigated	80	85	98
size of village capital fund (US$)	$600	$1,000	$2,000
average savings level per household	$20	$30	$40

The amounts and type of government aid vary according to
which category a village is in. Until 1975 more aid was
given to the 'independent' than to the 'basic' villages
to stimulate the basic villages to improve themselves.
In 1975 and 1976 more aid was channelled to the less
successful villages; but this change generated criticism
from the better-off villages, whose leaders complained
they were not being adequately rewarded for their
efforts, and subsequently the policy of 'incentives for
outstanding achievement' has been reintroduced. (The
proposed reform of canal management, as we shall see,
is an attempt to apply similar principles.)
    However, the instrument of government-orchestrated
competition is obviously inadequate for getting mass
compliance on a wide range of matters. Often what is
wanted by the township officials to enable them to ful-
fil their targets is not wanted by the farmers: for
example, rural drinking water supplies arranged in one
way rather than another, a fish pond (built to government specifications), roof improvements according to
government standards, adoption of a particular paddy
variety. The farmers know they are dependent on the
government administration for fertilisers, institutional
credit (both are monopolised by the NACF), registration
of land which they wish to bring under or take out of
cultivation, buying machinery, even for the success of
their children at school. Officials use this dependence
to coerce or bargain with farmers.
    Reed describes a common occurrence: 'Projects or
proposals are presented to village or farmers in the way
of demands and benefits are accorded as special gifts...
The normal method of operation is for a township level
official to call in or visit the village head and inform him of a project (e.g., Saemaul projects, joint
farm) or target (e.g., HYV, winter barley). The village

head then calls a meeting of household heads and presents
the demands with apologies. Long discussion may follow
with complaints and criticism openly voiced, but in the
end the required action is invariably taken' (1979, p.
136). Hence if physical coercion is not used, then a
varying combination of peer group pressure, shame, self-
interest and subtle control over access to farm commod-
ities and credit is the normal method.

The mobilising and directive efforts were carried
to an especially high pitch in the Saemaul Movement.
As described by anthropologist Vincent Brandt:

> Because of unrelenting pressure from the top,
> bureaucratic efforts to achieve the movement's
> goals were intense. Saemaul became the main focus
> of activity for all local administrative agencies,
> and thousands of other officials from the capital
> descended on the provinces to inspect, exhort,
> direct operations, and - to some extent - compete
> with local officials. The result initially was
> often confusion and bureaucratic overkill, while
> the astonished villagers struggled to comply with
> mounting and sometimes conflicting demands for
> compliance with various aspects of the overall
> plan (1977).

'Modernising' rural housing has been a particular
emphasis of the Saemaul Movement, especially in villages
in line of sight from national highways. Farmers have
been put under heavy and assorted pressures to take out
loans (twenty-five years at low interest) to have their
traditional house replaced by one built according to
one of a small number of Ministry of Home Affairs models,
in a style described by one observer as ' bastardisa-
tion of modern and rococo', [23] looking for all the
world like Mediterranean summer villas dropped down in
the Korean countryside. The replacement of baked-brick
garden walls, outhouses and ox sheds with structures to
Saemaul (concrete-intensive) specifications is part of
the same drive. Eyewitness accounts suggest the ex-
cesses to which the drive has been prone:

> If several farmers in a village were reluctant to
> replace the traditional brush fences around their
> houses with cement walls, jeep loads of men from
> the county seat might arrive and simply tear down
> all the brush fences. Similarly there were
> occasions when house owners who were unwilling
> to make the substantial investment necessary to
> replace their thatched roofs with composition or
> tile might return home from a market trip to find
> the thatch gone and their homes open to the sky
> (Brandt, 1977).

Again, when government wishes to improve an existing
small irrigation project and affiliate it to a FLIA, the
law says that two thirds of the intended beneficiaries
must give (voluntarily) their written approval. In
practice this requirement is often not met, because
farmers are wary of being brought into closer involvement with 'government' (as the FLIA is seen to be).
Officials normally do attempt to obtain written consent;
but if not, the project goes ahead anyway. In a recent
country-wide survey of 360 farmers in this situation,
27 percent said they had not signed the project contract
and 33 percent said they had signed involuntarily.[24]

Compliance on these matters is often intensely
resented by villagers, partly just because the material
cost to them is often high.[25] Often villages (or individual farmers) try to bargain with officials, by agree-
ing to do what the officials want in return for side-
benefits. But the promised side-benefits do not always
arrive, after the villagers have already built the fish
pond they did not want[26] or unwillingly taken out
expensive loans to change their house. The village
leaders are then often in an extremely stressful position.
Not surprisingly, a recent survey of over 500 farmers
found that a majority agreed that public officials cannot
be trusted, and agreed that the world is run by a few
powerful persons.[27]

Some of these points can be further illustrated in
the context of the campaign to spread HYVs. Korea has
had high-yielding Japonica rice varieties for decades,
but recently has bred somewhat higher-yielding varieties
(HYVs). Farmers have tended to resist their adoption,
however, partly on grounds of taste, partly because
their yield advantage over the best of the older
varieties seems small. We noted in the previous chapter
that whereas the government relied on economic incentives
in the early 1970s, the policy has changed since the
mid 1970s, and the economic incentives have since been
at best only slightly positive, and sometimes negative.
Reed reports (and my observations agree) that there is
now a 'widely held conviction among farmers that the
effort and cost of rice production is not matched by the
returns; at least not relative to returns to labor
observed outside agriculture. This feeling is summed up
in a recent farmers' saying: "Weep while tilling the
soil, weep again at harvest time, and weep once more at
the market place". A more measurable reflection of
problems with rice farming is the unprecedented, recent,
steady decline in the price of paddy land in Korea'(1979,
p.79). It is illegal for a farmer to move his land out
of rice into other crops without (infrequently granted)
government approval.

As economic incentives in favour of HYVs have weakened, the government has turned to various other methods. The yield competition we have already noted. Rice production, especially HYVs, is being strongly promoted via the educational channels of the New Community Movement, and thus is being connected to sacred nation-building objectives. The allocation of institutional credit (of which the NACF is the monopoly supplier) may be linked to proportion of area planted to HYVs. Targetry is also important. Before each season, the Ministry of Agriculture gives an indicative target on how much of each province's paddy area should be under HYVs. The province then sets target percentages for each FLIA within its jurisdiction. The FLIA breaks this down into targets for each village. 1978's target for SY FLIA was 81 percent. The responsibility of the FLIA's extension staff is then to try to ensure that each farmer grows at least 81 percent of his area under HYVs. They do not do so by helping the farmer to get the necessary inputs; this is the job of the ORD and NACF. Rather, they limit their efforts to persuading the farmer to sign a statement of intent, declaring that he will grow at least 81 percent of his paddy land under HYVs, and then display this piece of paper on the wall or gate of his house in a prominent place, thereby attempting to mobilise village pressures for conformity to the target.

In some extreme cases (reported in the press from all over the country)[28] ORD extension agents destroyed seedbeds planted to ordinary varieties and forced farmers to plant the recommended variety; or before the planting went to the house of a reluctuant farmer and removed his paddy seed while he was absent, replacing it with the favoured variety.

There is also some evidence that the very high levels of fertiliser consumption are being achieved through methods similar to those used to promote HYVs.[29] Fertiliser production in South Korea is in the hands of a small number of joint venture companies linking Korean and Western or Japanese firms. The government has guaranteed them high profit levels in return for high production quotas. The government is then responsible for the sale of the fertiliser, through the NACF. Farmers are commonly made to sign promissory notes to pay for the fertiliser after the harvest - but without knowing the price per unit. Strong efforts are made by local agents to persuade them to use large quantities, perhaps bargaining more fertiliser use for improved access to credit.

Still another component of the HYV strategy is the 'joint farm'. In the late 1960s the South Korean government initiated a programme to encourage contiguous

farmers to form five to ten hectare blocks to be farmed
with joint management and labour, while retaining
private property rights in the land. These farms were
to be made the focus of intensive extension efforts.
The statistics indicate that the number of joint farms
increased dramatically from 500 in 1968 to over 50,000
in 1976, covering 60 percent of all the paddy land in
South Korea. Reed's study of two localities found that
most of the joint farms existed on paper only.

> Township guidance officials had gone out to each
> village and through consultation with the village
> head obtained a list of farmers' names to place
> on a mimeographed agreement prepared in advance.
> These agreements were then filed in the township
> office and a report of 100 percent fulfilment of
> the joint farm target sent up to the county and
> national levels. In many cases the farmers them-
> selves were not even aware that their names had
> been used and no joint activities were carried
> out (1979, p.205).

However, some joint farms were set up - and in these
cases the management was taken over completely by the
extension agents, so as to ensure that their demonstration and yield targets were met; they regarded the
farmers as mere suppliers of labour. The farmers,
according to Reed,[30] responded by seeing the joint farm
as wholly to do with the government, not with them, so
that instead of providing them with experience of joint
management, it reinforced the pattern of dependency and
passivity in the face of government.

However, passivity is not always the reaction, as
the following illustrates. In this case, a group of
farmers had land in a 300 hectare block fed from a
small reservoir, near a major highway along which
frequently travelled a senior official of the Ministry
of Agriculture. The latter decided that the farmers
must be told to begin transplanting their paddy from
the tail-end and work up towards the top, instead of
from top to tail as the farmers had always done; the
former being thought more efficient. The order came
down. The ORD officials and the township officials put
heavy pressure on the farmers to comply. The farmers,
feeling that their very lifeblood was being tampered
with, arose as one and marched on the township office.
The township chief, rather than face their anger, fled.
The order w as dropped, and that was the end of the
matter.

This incident is however unusual, in that the
farmers resisted successfully, and relatedly, they
acted collectively. For a further technique of state

control is that groups larger than single villages are
not brought together. The bargaining we have noted takes
place between officials and individuals or at most single
villages. In this way issues are individuated, the power
structure is personalised, and manifestations of generalised opposition to government policies are prevented.
What aggregation of farmers' interests and grievances
takes place is done by the officials themselves - and
one recalls the observation quoted earlier that, 'There
is some flow of information from the villages that is
fed back into the administrative decision-making process,
but it is probably minimal'.

Officials may privately criticise the central government policies they are charged with carrying out.
Privately they may talk of central government's 'showbusiness', its 'credit policy' - the latter meaning not
its policy on loans, but its tendency to choose projects
which will ostentatiously reflect 'credit' on the government (one example of which, according to FLIA officials,
is the government's willingness to make funds available
for new irrigation facilities but not for improvement of
existing ones, the latter being less good for gaining
'credit'). But they feel themselves powerless to do
other than carry out orders. The township chief who
fled his office in the earlier incident told my informant
that he knew perfectly well there was no good reason to
make the farmers transplant from the tail-end first - but
he saw no alternative but to get it implemented. (The
determination of Koreans in administrative hierarchies
to carry out orders from 'authority' is often noted by
foreign observers, and perhaps helps to explain why the
instrument of plan 'targets' seems to be unusually
effective in Korea as a technique of motivation.)

Yet the words used to describe and name the institutions of government consistently carry connotations of
a quite different kind. The county (gun) is described
as the 'local autonomous body' - but has little autonomy.
The National Agricultural Cooperative Federation is in
no sense a federation of cooperatives - there are no
cooperatives to be federated, and the oganisation is
tightly directed from the centre.[31] The New Community
Movement is described as a 'popular, self-help, and
socio-economic reform movement initiated voluntarily by
people in the 1970s with the ultimate goal of modernisation and peaceful unification of the country'
(Minister of Home Affairs, 1972, p.108); in fact it was
initiated and is sustained and directed from the centre,
and had the effect of pre-empting independent local
leadership by making the village leadership highly responsive to the centre, complementing the dependence of
farmers on central agencies for resources.[32] And of
course we have the example of the Hueng Nong Gye, with

their place in the statistics and organisation charts but not on the ground.

A final point. The South Korean government has used many of the same techniques of control and compliance in its industrial interventions as in agriculture. The technique of the competition, for example, has been adopted to promote(industrial) exports. On 'Export Day', 30 November, the highest ranking exporters are with great fanfare awarded 'industrial merit medals' of gold, silver and bronze pagoda rank. In addition, special awards are given to thoseexporting over US$ 100 million worth of goods. The prizes are awarded by President Park personally, and are much coveted.[33] The technique of using an enterprise's dependence on government-controlled inputs to secure its compliance in other contexts is also familiar. South Korean firms are dependent to an unusual degree (by international comparison) on credit for recurrent and investment purposes, and credit is tightly controlled by government (a private banking sector exists in name but not in practice). The government uses its control of credit (also foreign exchange) to enforce highly discretionary commands over individual firms or clusters of firms - for example, commands to import less from country X, or invest in a huge shipyard, or contribute more to the national defence fund, etc. Knowledge that the government can cut off the credit at any time is often sufficient to elicit the desired response. The threat need only be carried out occasionally.[34]

CONCLUSION

In short, the broader context of irrigator-system relations in South Korea is one in which rural government institutions pre-empt to the extent possible the personal decisions that farmers must make, so as to ensure their continued support for the larger political body of which they are an important component.[35] Given this, the absence of any formal role for farmers in the decisions of the FLIA is not surprising; though the indifference towards informing,the farmers collectively of water policies and other features of the FLIA, as manifested in the SY Public Newspaper, does illustrate graphically how far the exclusion of farmers as a collective interest group goes; as also does the hidden SuggestionsBox in the HQ building, and the farmer's comment that the farmers saw the FLIA staff as 'just tax collectors'.

By excluding farmers as a group, the FLIA ensures that relations between FLIA and farmers are through personal contact; the power structure is thus personalised. In this context both staff and farmers tend

to see individual or village 'problems', not general
'issues' (with the major exception of the water charge),
and generalised complaints are not raised - or raised
only at the discretion of the staff. In addition, the
transmission of an implicit assumption that 'the FLIA
knows best' is facilitated in this kind of power structure. The same points apply to the structure of government-farmer relations more generally. One would expect
to find at the twice yearly meetings between Field
Station staff and HNG leaders (the one context where
generalised criticism of FLIA policies might be expressed)
much emphasis on (a) the wisdom of the FLIA staff, and
(b) feelings of community between staff and farmers, to
foster a common sense of local attachment and content-
ment, and to reinforce HNG leaders' identification with
the FLIA. At the same time it is clear from farmers'
comments (such as,   'the farmers don't trust the
FLIA') that such techniques have not been entirely
successful: many farmers, on the contrary, feel critical
of the FLIA and of their own exclusion, but feel muzzled -
until they approach the question from the 'special
national security problem' of South Korea, which leads
them to confer more legitimacy on their exclusion than
they do in other contexts. This analysis of the specific
context of the FLIA thus helps us to understand the
nature of the relative political 'stability' in rural
South Korea; though one should not lose sight of the
real improvements in living standards which have taken
place, as a non-coercive[36] influence on that stability.
     Yet as we have seen, those real improvements in
living standards have themselves been brought about with
often heavy use of coercion. It would be interesting to
examine in detail the contribution of coercive agricultural extension to the high levels of agricultural
productivity now prevailing. The big improvements in
paddy yields which occurred during the Japanese colonial
period were effected with scant regard for farmers'
participation; if the farmers did not follow the extension
agents' orders, the police might be brought in. Against
this background, the post-Independence methods have
been relatively benign. Even so, one can already see
the dangers of the overwhelming drive by government
officials for agricultural and rural modernisation, not
only in terms of the build-up of resentments but also
in more economic terms. Some of the seed varieties
most forcefully promoted by government have been deci-
mated by pests and diseases, a result of quite inadequate
pre-testing (which takes time). While the government
has successfully brought about the adoption of a formid-
able array of modern, energy intensive inputs, there are
suggestions that the chemical composition of the soil is
suffering as a result,[37] and it is likely that both
irrigation water, which is used for household washing,

and drinking water are becoming polluted (drinking water
via seepage into drinking water reservoirs), with possibly severe and as yet unmeasured effects on health.[38]
The heavy use of these inputs (and of large irrigation
pumps where water could if better managed flow by gravity
alone) also worsens the country's already heavy dependence
on imported petroleum, thereby partially offsetting the
advantages of cereal self-sufficiency.

To answer the question of this chapter we have had
to go well beyond the specifics of irrigation and examine
government-populace relations more generally. In the
next chapter discussion of the mode of internal operation
of the FLIA will also lead us away from irrigation as
such towards the organisation of the public bureaucracy
more generally, and specifically to the issue of how the
central government attempts to control its local parastatal agencies and the responses of the latter to these
attempts.

NOTES

1. 'Water use efficiency' here refers to technical
efficiency, the ratio of the volume of water used for
crop production to the volume of water diverted from (or
stored at) the source. 'Water productivity' refers to
the ratio of the quantity of production (e.g. tons/ha.)
to the quantity of water used (e.g. cubic metres/ha.).
Phrases such as 'efficient use of water' sometimes refer
to the latter, production-oriented notion of efficiency.
2. Levine et al, 1976.
3. In the wealthier parts of cities, the household
representative is not infrequently the maid.
4. At New Year he is paid the small sum of 14,000 won
as a contribution to expenses.
5. This is the Manager's statement on 'Save irrigation water even when it is sufficient'. 'It is easy to
neglect the saving of irrigation water these days. But
rainfall is not reliable, so we have to prepare for when
it fails. Whenever I go about the canals I see that
some farmers are breaking the drainage stop-mud and
letting all the water drain out of the field. They will
regret it if drought comes. If drought comes, farmers
fight each other to fill their paddies first. Every
farmer should stick to an order of water supply, based
on the principles of scientific watering. Fighting
between farmers is one of the factors that destroys the
spirit of the New Community Movement. So everyone should
cease to fight for water out of order. We have already
completed irrigation projects which will ensure that even
in a serious drought we can supply water to the Benefit
Area in transplanting and growing season. In this
situation if we fail to supply water the main responsib-

ility will fall on the farmers. So I insist that every farmer should not break down the paddy drain in the rainy season, and should keep up the water level in the paddies on rainy days.

Our government is now in a difficult situation because of the oil shock. So to keep our standard of living rising we must save irrigation water as part of the conservation movement. Now I am going to prepare a plan against severe drought.' July 1979.

6. See for example Abel 1975, quoted below.

7. The Taiwanese side of the comparison is based on my own impressions from talking to officials of the Chianan Irrigation Association, and from a private communication from A. Bottrall on irrigation management in Taiwan.

8. A total of 6,300,000 won was spent in 1978 on prizes in these competitions (including those for Field Stations).

9. Though the cult of the Leader is not carried as far as it is in North Korea. See Cumings 1974.

10. Dong-il Kim 1980, E-4.

11. Brandt and Lee 1977, p.29, and Pak and Gamble 1975. Reed (1979), speaking of decision-making within villages, reports, 'Decisions are arrived at only after thorough (often interminable) discussion when all can voice an opinion, though the views of the natural leaders are usually given more weight' (130). '...village affairs are never conducted in an authoritarian manner; leaders act more as moderators than as decision-makers or executives' (132). However Reed also makes clear that participation is, as one would expect, shaped by class position; the heads of landless or near-landless households take little part even in deliberations about forming a cooperative labor exchange group, which vitally affect their interests (1979, p.180).

12. Pak and Gamble 1975, p.44, Steinberg 1980, p.G-4

13. Pak and Gamble 1975, p.46-51.

14. According to Brandt and Lee 1977, common village organisations include: the 4-H Club, Children and Mothers' Club, Village Development Fund, New Community Movement Fund, Roof Improvement Fund, Forestry Fund. There have also been various kinds of youth associations, such as the Reconstruction Youth Association, with village branches. See also Reed 1979, p.134-43.

15. Brandt and Lee 1977, p.131.

16. Henderson 1968; but for a somewhat different interpretation see Cumings 1974a.

17. Brandt and Lee 1977.

18. Pak and Gamble 1975.

19. One needs to know more about who is selected, and how, for the various formal leadership roles in each village, specifically to know the relative importance of the HNG leader.

20. A 1969 survey showed that only 10 percent of the rural household heads in the survey visited the myon office more than 5 times a year. A survey of four villages in the same area in 1976 showed that in all four villages the corresponding figure was over 50 percent. (Brandt and Lee 1977, p.60).

21. For example, the July 1979 issue has approximately half of the 12 (small) pages devoted to these latter topics (national flag etiquette, South Korean politics, and anti-North Korean sentiment).

22. The section which follows on the New Community Movement is based on Brandt and Lee 1977, also Acqua 1974.

23. Steinberg 1980, p.G-1

24. Dong-il Kim 1980, p.E-4.

25. Reed 1979, p.136, describes one case in detail. I heard of many cases of similar kind.

26. Reed reports from his study area, 'cement fish ponds measuring about eighty by thirty feet and eight feet deep were constructed in a large number of villages early in the Saemaul drive [on instructions from government officials]. Not one of these was being used in 1977 and they merely collected water and were considered a hazard. Villagers considered the return on raising fish to be below the production cost ' (1979, p.94,n.4).

27. Dong-il Kim 1980, p.E-4. The source does not give the size of the majority.

28. Reed 1979, pp. 80, 99 n.32 gives examples from 1977 and 1978. Similar incidents were being reported by agricultural economists working with farmers in 1979.

29. Reed 1979, p.80, Kim Chang Soo 1977, Park U.S. 1978.

30. Reed 1979, p.235.

31. The NACF Annual Report 1977 describes in general terms the aims and objectives of the NACF without mentioning the role of farmers or without defining 'members'. On such matters it confines itself to generalities like, '...agricultural cooperatives are farmers' voluntary organisations to promote agricultural production and to elevate their living standard through a close cooperation under the spirit of mutual self-help among them' (p.8).

32. Acqua 1974.

33. Jones and SaKong 1978, Chp. 4, p.25.

34. Jones and SaKong 1978, Chp.4.

35. Acqua 1974.

36. 'Non-coercive' is used to differentiate this influence on political stability from those – including coercion and ideological persuasion – which have been more directly manipulated by the regime.

37. Kim Chang Soo 1977.

38. Steinberg et al 1980.

6
Sy Flia as Government Bureaucracy and Social Group

On the one hand the farmers are excluded from the FLIA; on the other, the FLIA is closely regulated by the government via its legal status as a public corporation. The government (specifically, the Ministry of Agriculture) sets conditions of service, staffing scales, salary scales, budget and account procedures, rules for assessing water charges, and the like. The framework of rules and regulations are uniform for all FLIAs in the country; and with respect to terms of employment and budget procedures, are somewhat different from those of government ministries and their sub-national agencies (like the ORD). Further the FLIAs, but not the latter, can enter into contracts, acquire property, sue and be sued, and in other ways manifest a separate legal existence - subject always to the Minister of Agriculture being able by law to give to any FLIA whatever directions he deems fit.

Variable, discretionary control is exercised in two main ways: appointment of the President, and scrutiny of the budget.

In the Ministry of Agriculture is a bureau concerned to monitor the FLIAs operational activities (as distinct from construction activities, for which there is a separate bureau). But the central government's bureau is small (fifteen staff), and the detailed monitoring and control is carried out from a special bureau of each provincial administration for FLIAs in that province.

Appointment of the Presidents of the twenty-two largest FLIAs (with a command area of 5,000 hectares or more) is made after close consultation between the provincial and central government bureaus, the appointment being made formally by the Minister of Agriculture. [1] For smaller FLIAs the appointment is made by the provincial governor on recommendation of the (government-appointed) head of the county administration. A strong effort is made to appoint people who are 'natives' of the command area and own land within it. In virtually all of the twenty-two

largest the Presidents are career civil servants nearing
retirement age, who retire prematurely from the civil
service to take the job of President (in a four year
term).   SY's current President, for example, comes from
the SY area and his family have land there; but he
himself has spent most of his working life in the Ministry
of Agriculture in Seoul. By taking the post of
President he gained an additional two years beyond the
compulsory retirement age as well as an increase in
salary. Whether posts such as the FLIA Presidentship
are used as 'dumping grounds' for eliminating competitors
for the few senior posts within the central government
service is not clear. Certainly the prestige of
Ministry jobs, in Seoul, is much greater than equivalent
rank jobs in FLIAs, in the provinces, which reflects
the centuries-old tradition of government centralisation.
      The budget scrutiny and sanction of each FLIA follows
similar lines to the appointment of the President, except
that the planned budgets of all one hundred and twenty
two FLIAs have to be approved by the Ministry of
Agriculture as well as by the provincial government.
At either level, changes in a FLIA's budget can be
ordered.   This is coupled with a set of stringent
arrangements for inspection and audit. Not only are
documents sent to the provincial and central administra-
tions for audit, but each year between November and
January three separate inspections - intended as
investigations of a police nature - take place; one by
the Ministry of Agriculture, a second by the provincial
administration, a third by the Board of Audit. Each
team consists of three to five persons, and normally
(in the case of SY) takes about a week checking records,
operations, materials and property, and examining any
part of the organisation it sees fit to.   (It was on the
orders of one such inspection team that the former
section of Agricultural Extension was closed down, and
its functions taken on by the Canal and Pump Operation
section.)   On top of this, there are surprise inspections
(three in the past five years at SY).
      What financial discretion is open to the FLIA lies
(legally) entirely with the President.   No-one is
authorised to spend money without his prior approval,
and specifically not the heads of Field Stations. As
one said, 'If we want to buy even so much as an ash
tray for our room we have to ask the President's
permission first'.   In an emergency, if for example a
breach is threatening and the President is not available,
the head of Finance Section is authorised to give approval
but it is a responsibility he wishes to avoid.
      The President also controls promotions (which we
consider later), including the appointment of his deputy,
the Manager, though his decision on the Manager must be
approved by the provincial administration. Promotion from

grade four to three depends on success in an examination
set and marked by the provincial administration - but
the President decides who is allowed to sit the
examination.   On the other hand, it is the provincial
administration's FLIA bureau, not the President, which
decides which successful candidates in the entry
examination at grade five should go to which FLIA.
     The principle means of control over the FLIAs by
government, then, are (1) the appointment of the
President, (2) the structure of authority within the
FLIA which concentrates it in the President, (3) control
over the budget through the requirement for prior
approval and annual audit, (4) regular and irregular
government inspections of operations, property and
records, (5) determination of the terms and conditions
of employment, and perhaps, (6) influence over who is
'successful' in the recruitment examinations.

TERMS AND CONDITIONS OF EMPLOYMENT

     Recruitment is by two routes: direct hiring, and
examination.   Direct hiring is used for temporary and
permanent 'employees', examination is used for entry
to the professional positions.   Until roughly 1973 the
common pattern was for a young man to join as a
temporary employee (hired by the President), get
promotion to permanent employee, then after perhaps ten
years from the time of joining sit the examination for
grade 5.   Since 1973 the proportion of grade 5 staff
who enter directly via the examination route rather than
via promotion of employees has been rising, and with this
an increase in the proportion of graduates of two year,
post-high school technical colleges.   But no minimum
educational qualification is needed to sit the entry
examination to grade 5.   The examination is set by the
provincial administration on behalf of the FLIAs in the
province, and marked by the provincial administration's
special examination staff.   The National Agricultural
Federation and the Organisation for Rural Development
have their own entry examinations, set and marked by the
same provincial office.
     Candidates are asked their preferred postings, but
which FLIA a successful candidate is sent to is decided
by the provincial government. Officially at least, the
FLIA has no influence over which candidates it gets.
But it is generally accepted that a candidate should be
posted to the FLIA nearest his home, and this generally
corresponds to the candidate's own wishes; there is a
strong 'native place' preference.   Virtually all will
have their home in the same province; only for senior
technician positions may a person from another province
be recruited, a restriction which reflects feelings of
provincial rivalry.

Competition for posts available at SY FLIA is keen.
Ratios of fourteen candidates for one grade 5 administrative post, and eight for one technical post, are common.
SY's province has an unusally large number of agricultural
high schools and two year agricultural colleges, however,
whose graduates regard the FLIAs as one obvious source
of secure employment.

Once recruited (especially if to grade 5), the
person looks on the FLIA as his lifetime employment.
Transfer to another FLIA is rare, and still more so is
transfer to another agency such as the Organisation for
Rural Development or the National Agricultural
Cooperatives Federation; the FLIAs are not ladders into
the provincial or central government. Most of what
out-flow does take place occurs in the lower grades, as
young men leave to go into private business (perhaps
succeeding their father). Amongst the 'employees',
on the other hand, turnover is much higher - especially,
as expected, amongst the temporaries.

Salary scales give relatively heavy weight to length
of service. Virtually the same absolute annual increments
are used for all grades (and therefore are a declining part
of income the higher the grade). The weightage is
such that a grade 4 man with six years' service will earn
less than a grade 5 man with more than ten years of
service; or more strikingly, an unusally fast promoted
grade 3 with ten years service will receive less than a
grade 5 with twenty-one years' service or more - a
functionary with supervisory responsibilities will get
less than an operative with just over twice as many years
of service.

As between grade 5 and 'employee' there is little
difference in salary. A first category employee with
six years' service receives 110,000 won a month, a grade
5 with the same length of service receives 127,000 won
a month. But whereas length of service increments for
employees stop after the tenth year, graded staff go on
receiving such increments until they retire. [2]

Within the professional scale the range from bottom
to top is relatively small. Taking only rank-related
payments the ratio of grade 5 to grade 3 (section head)
is 1:1.6, and of grade 5 to Manager, 1:2.2. However
there is a distinct break between Manager and President:
in SY's case, the President gets over 25 percent more
(including the Manager's length of service payment).
This reflects the sharply differing statuses of President
and Manager: the President is the government's agent
sent in from outside (almost never is the President a
promotee), the Manager is a man who has come up through
the ranks of the FLIA. In æ highly centralised a state
as South Korea, this difference is marked by a large
jump in salary, and by various other symbols of
authority, notably a chauffeur and luxuriously

upholstered jeep for the President's use. However, in
s mall FLIAs one would not expect the same symbolic and
material differentiation; the dividing line is
probably between the twenty two largest whose
Presidents are appointed by the Minister of Agriculture,
and the others whose Presidents are appointed by the
provincial governor.   (The salary of the President
depends on the area of the FLIA, as given in a special
Ministry of Agriculture scale for FLIA Presidents).

However, staff other than the President are on a
scale (uniform for all FLIAs in the country) which gives
them more than central government staff of equivalent
rank at levels below the rank of FLIA bureau chief (next
below Manager).   For example, a FLIA grade 5 with four
years' service gets 120,000 won a month, the equivalent
Ministry of Agriculture grade 5b with four years' service
gets 118,000 a month.   Even at bureau chief level
(grade 2), a FLIA man gets little less than his
Ministry rank equivalent (a FLIA grade 2 with ten years'
service gets 220,000 a month, an equivalent Ministry 3b
with ten years gets 230,000 a month).   (Central
government employees have no special allowances, such as
a dearness allowance for Seoul.)   The FLIA scale gives
more weight to length of service than does the Ministry
scale, which emphasises rank (intended to reflect merit).
Both FLIA and Ministry scales are less than that for the
big public corporations, such as the Agricultural
Development Corporation, the national canal investigation,
design and construction organisation.   It is said that
generally speaking private companies pay the most, then
national parastatals like the Agricultural Development
Corporation, then local parastatals like the FLIAs, then
the civil service (in the lower, numerically preponderant
ranks).   On both sides the relatively low level of civil
service salaries is explained in terms of the offsetting
advantages of having more power and status.   Ministry
of Agriculture officials are prone to refer disparagingly
to FLIA staff as of 'degraded quality'. No one in their
right mind would think of transferring from a low rank
in the Ministry of Agriculture to a FLIA in order to get
a higher salary.

FLIA staff get the same medical, retirement and
holiday benefits as government employees. They pay a
percentage of their salary into a medical insurance
scheme for government and public sector employees, the
amount is matched by the employer, and they receive most
of the costs of medical care if injured on the job. [3]
Paid leave includes the sixteen national holidays, plus
five days' vacation, plus sickness and compassionate leave
up to a maximum of twenty days including the five days'
vacation.   At retirement a lump sum is paid, its size
depending on length of service and salary at retirement; [4]
there is no pension.

STAFF ASSESSMENT

Once a year the head of each bureau writes a
performance report on each graded staff member who
falls within that bureau, and the head of each section
writes a similar report on each temporary and permanent
employee in his section. So, for example, the head
of the Management bureau writes reports on all Technical
graded staff in the Field Stations (based on advisory
reports by the head of the Field Station). No
performance report is written on the patrollers - it is
assumed that if they don't do their job adequately the
village chief and HNG leader will not renominate them,
or that by other means their poor performance will come
to the Field Station head, who will not reappoint them.
At the upper end of the hierarchy, no reports are written
on grade 2 staff or above (bureau heads, Manager,
President).
The reports are written on and follow the lay-out
of a complex form, a separate form for each grade. For
grade three the headings are as follows:

1. Work output   (10)
        Quantity   (5)
        Quality   (5)

2. Performance capacity   (6)
        Knowledge   (2)
        Judgement and leadership   (2)
        Personality   (2)

3. Work attitude   (4)
        Willingness to take responsibility, (2)
        cooperativeness
        Faithfulness   (2)

The reporter has to comment under each heading.
The numbers in brackets refer to points. I now
describe the points system in some detail, despite its
complexity, to illustrate the striking difference between
the elaborate codification of such matters as personnel
policy, and the undefined state of the main operational
activities of the FLIA, which we noted in Chapter 4.
First of all, it is necesssary to bear in mind that
the points system applies only to graded staff, not to
employees or patrollers; so that well over half the
total staff of the FLIA is excluded. Promotion of the
employees to grade 5 is now by written examination, but
until 1973 was at the discretion of the President.
Amongst graded staff, each person's total score is
the sum of length of service points and merit points.
Length of service points are weighted by the factor of
0.6, merit points by 0.4. Length of service thus counts

more than merit not only for salary (as noted earlier) but
also for points for promotion between grades.

To begin with length of service: A person must stay
in each grade for a stipulated minimum period (one year
in grade 5, 2½ years in grade 4, 3 years in grade 3, etc).
Each month of service within this period earns 0.62
points. Each month within one to twenty-four months in
excess of the minimum earns 0.13; each month within
twenty-four to forty-eight months in excess of the
minimum earns 0.09, and beyond forty-eight months in the
same grade, no points are earned. Thus, to build up
points beyond those given by forty-eight months of
service in addition to the minimum service for that
grade, the merit component must be increased.

The merit component includes three sub-components:
Points are awarded to each individual by the writer of
his annual report (the head of his bureau), by the
Manager, and by the President, and their verdicts are
averaged; each evaluator follows the headings on the
report form (the numbers in brackets are the maximum
points under each heading and subheading.) Then are
added points for in-service training (there are no
points for educational qualifications), calculated as
follows: at the end of each training course is an
examination; the percentage score in this exam is
weighted by the factor of 0.02 and the figure added to
the merit total - hence in-service training is a useful
way of amassing promotion points. The third sub-component
is for 'other' sources of merit - mainly special prizes,
which may be for job performance, public service of some
kind (charity or political work), or valour. (For
instance, in the interests of promoting agricultural
mechanisation President Park recently awarded special
prizes to the heads of Agricultural Machinery sections
of the FLIAs which, like SY, had been especially
vigorous in this field.) Any award from President Park
counts as 3 points, one from the Prime Minister, 2.5,
from the Minister of Agriculture, 2 points, the
provincial governor, 1.5, the President of the FLIA, 1
point.

By this formula an individual's point total is
calculated. Individuals are meant to be promoted in the
order of their points, and on promotion to the next grade
their points then go to zero. However, individuals do
not know what their total is; this is a secret closely
guarded by the head of the Personnel section, shared
only with his superiors. This means that the President
has considerable de facto discretion about the order of
promotion. Moreover, between grades 4 and 3 promotion is
by examination (set and marked by the provincial
administration); but the President decides who is
allowed to sit the examination.

The head of Personnel says that he spends much of his

time keeping individuals' scores up to date.

The promotion ladders are narrow. The whole Administration side constitutes one ladder (people can transfer from Finance to Budget to Personnel); but Agricultural Affairs and Engineering are separate ladders, between which transfer is possibly only after successful performance in a provincial examination (and rare in practice). The number of posts allowable at each grade on each ladder is set by the Ministry, depending on the FLIA's command area. The Ministry also stipulates what percentage of the staff on each ladder can have various levels of merit points (for example, only 10 percent can have between thirty-seven points and forty points, 30 percent have between twenty- nine and thirty-six points, etc.). The FLIA has further stipulated that of the nine grade 3 Field Station posts, five must be assigned to administrators, four to technicians (though does not try to say which Field Station should be headed by an administrator, which by a technician).

This latter ruling is a focus for the sense of grievance felt by technical people towards administrative staff. Although there are many more technical (graded) staff than administrators (sixty-one to thirty-eight), at senior levels (grade 3 and above) there are as many administrators as technicians, which means that a grade 5 technical man has a much smaller chance of getting to a senior grade than a grade 5 administrator. Technical people throw up their hands in a gesture of futility: 'it is unjust, but that's the way things are in Korea, administrators rule'.

With narrow promotion ladders and little mid-career outflow, promotion tends to be slow - especially for technical staff, and especially between grade 4 (operative status) and grade 3 (supervisory status). Waits at grade 4 of ten years or more are common, and promotees from the ranks of permanent employees (the only route to the graded posts before 1973) may expect only a short period as a grade 3 before compulsory retirement at age fifty-five, now that many new young recruits are going straight to grade 5 via the examination route. On the other hand, the heavy weighting of length of service in salary helps compensate those who fail to get up the promotion ladder.

One study of Korean local administration reports that in general personal connections, obligations, reciprocity (called baek, from the English, 'background') are very important for individuals' success. 5 It would be interesting to know more about how these promotion procedures are actually used in the FLIA, about how much promotion selection is the result of personal connections with the President and senior staff, and how much selection is indeed - as the complex rules and

formulae seem intended to have people believe - highly
bureaucratised.

As for punishment, there are again highly elaborate
codes of procedures which have to be followed in
disciplining a staff member, set by the Ministry.
There are three main degrees: private rebuke from the
President; withholding of salary (up to one third);
and dismissal. (There may also be a public rebuke at a
FLIA-wide meeting.) At each stage the sanctioning
procedures differ; and dismissal can occur only after
a committee of senior staff have investigated. Nevertheless, it is reported that in the past five years,
five graded staff and two permanent employees have been
dismissed from service at SY FLIA (on what grounds is
not clear).

It is likely that transfer from one office and job
to another is also used to punish and reward. Staff
are to remain in any one job for a maximum of three
years, and the average is substantially less. Movement
between HQ and Field Station is common. Transfer
decisions are in the hands of the President.

FORMALISATION

The FLIA's life is governed, or meant to be governed,
by the regulations laid out in a thick manual prepared
by the Ministry of Agriculture. Its black cover and gold
lettered title, 'Farmland Improvement Associations:
Regulations', make it a conspicuous feature of the
(otherwise nearly empty) desk of any grade 3 person.
It sets out in elaborate detail budgetary and accounting
procedures, staffing and salary scales, job description
for each graded position, promotion rules and points
scales, punishment procedures, even the pro forma to be
used in reports from Station offices to HQ and the
proper frequency of meetings between FLIA staff at
different levels; and all matters relating to the
FLIA's connections with provincial and central
government.

This drive for formalisation and standardisation
helps account for the strong impression one gets on one's
first visit to SY FLIA of an organisation in well-ordered
control of its staff and environment. The HQ building
(a strictly functional two storied rectangle, approached
via an unsealed circular drive enclosing ill-kept
ornamental shrubs) displays in the foyer a framed
organisational chart of the FLIA, a notice board on which
is written meteorological information, and another giving
the names of those on radio station duty. As an
outsider, one will be taken upstairs to meet the President
and then to the Conference Room to be briefed. The
President's room is austere, with little sign of
occupancy. On the walls are the obligatory photograph

of President Park, an organisation chart of the FLIA, and
another of the Ministry of Agriculture (this latter
symbolising the closeness of the link with central
government). The large desk displays several telephones
but no trace of papers. In the corner, a South Korean
flag. A large sofa and two deep armchairs around a
small table complete the furnishings. The Conference
Room contains a long polished table with leather-
upholstered chairs, and around the walls impressive
displays of data and a relief map. The relief map uses
electric lights to mark the location of the various
facilities (blue for reservoirs, red for pump stations).
On a stand is a large folder, on each page of which is
written for the benefit of the visitor a main point to
be made in the briefing to follow. At the end the
visitor is presented with a glossy brochure titled (in
English as well as Korean) 'SY Farmland Improvement
Association: The Present State', with a colour photo
of a reservoir on the cover, and inside a succinct
account (in Korean) of the organisation's History,
Purpose, Activities, Organisation, Map, details on
structures, area irrigated, etc. He will also be
given a wall pennant saying, 'In commemoration of your
visit, SY FLIA' (in Korean and English). It may be
that only the twenty-two largest FLIAs have such tokens
to distribute.
    The arrangement of the offices gives a similar
impression of order, control, efficiency, and hierarchy.
The offices are two open-plan rooms opening on either
side of the entrance foyer, about twenty metres long, one
for the Administration bureau, the other for the
bureaus of Management and Land Development. About thirty
people work in each room. Upstairs are the offices
of the President, the Manager, the Conference Room, and
the Assembly Room (rarely used), with its row of
prize certificates awarded to the FLIA. In the open-
plan offices the desks are laid out in blocks, sides
and fronts touching, one block per section. At the
head of each block facing down the line is the desk of
the section chief. That of the bureau chief stands
apart. It is of wood, displays prominently a name and
position in gold lettering, and three or four telephones;
otherwise the top is bare. In front are four armchairs
and a small table where visitors are received. The
bureau chief's chair is a large, high backed swivel
armchair upholstered in imitation black leather,
equipped with a cane back support. The section head's
desk has one telephone, no name and position sign, and
may have one or two seats nearby for visitors. The
back of his chair is less high than the bureau chief's,
the arms thinner, the upholstery meaner, and it lacks
the cane back support. And so on down the line, the
desks and chairs more strictly functional and

uncomfortable with each one, the stacks of files and
papers getting higher, and by and large, the occupants
getting younger.

A similar impression of order and hierarchy is
given by the Field Station offices. There are only two
rooms, one for the Station head, the other for the rest
(and a cubicle for the radio station). On the walls
of the Station head's office are various charts on which
the results of key rice operations within the Section
are tabulated, together with maps and framed certificates
awarding the Station office a place in one of the several
inter-station competitions (notably, water charge
collection). In the main room are more maps, charts
from the Ministry of Agriculture showing rice pests,
the stages of rice growth and water requirement at each
stage, and other agronomic information. Each of the
graded staff will have a list of their individual duties,
which is derived from the book of FLIA regulations but
tailored to their own situation; each employee will
have a copy of the list of duties pertinent to his
category; and the patrollers have nothing.

The following reports are to be sent from each
Field Station to HQ during the irrigation season:

Technical

Subject	Frequency
1. Gauges	Telephoned/transmitted daily, register sent every 10 days
2. Request for permission to use pump station	Every time pump station to be used
3. Pump Station use	Every 10 days
4. Pest and disease control	" " "
5. " " " "	" " "
6. Conferences, lectures to farmers on pest and disease control	Weekly
7. Stocks of sprays	Every 10 days
8. Non-chemical fertiliser	" " "
9. Level of acidity in paddy fields	" " "
10. Paddy varieties (ha.)	Start of season
11. Harvesting of paddy (ha.)	Every 5 days during season
12. Land preparation (ha.)	Every 10 days during season
13. Paddy yields	End of season
14. Barley yields	" " "
15. Farming of 'special vegetables'	Every 10 days
16. Miscellaneous	

Administrative

Subject	Frequency
1. Staff attendance register	Monthly
2. Salaries claim	"
3. Patrollers' work register	"
4. Radio night duty register	"
5. Night duty meals register	"
6. Travel claims	"
7. Electricity account	"
8. Newspaper account	"
9. Hospitality account	"
10. Radio code account	"
11. Radio use	"
12. Field station head's office inspection report	Weekly
13. Conservation of the environment	Six monthly
14. " " "	" "
15. Radio inspection report	" "
16. Station head's Saemaul report	Three monthly
17. Station head's report on each staff member	Yearly

Back at HQ the information in these reports is aggregated and summarised in tables for the senior management. By the desk of the head of the Management bureau is a large data display board titled: "Increasing Rice Yields: 250 days' Operation Board", and seven tables, one for each step in rice production and another for 'barley seeds and sprays', each table giving the results for that step from each Field Station. Other wall tables by the Management head's desk include ones for the amount to be spent in each Field Station's area for pump station and canal maintenance. If one wishes one can also see the registers in which are tabulated much of the other information obtained from the Field Stations (the most incomplete of those I looked at were the gauge readings in various parts of the canals). In addition, the FLIA produces a forty-two page mimeographed booklet giving the guiding principles ('unity of purpose, faith and diligence, kindness and service'), the golden rules of maintenance ('do modernisation in the spring and autumn, get pumps and hoses ready in case of drought, make the Hueng Nong Gye keep the channels free of weed and silt'), other mottoes and slogans; and also elaborate details on SY's history, staffing, facilities, past and planned budget, maintenance programme. The FLIA also produces another mimeographed booklet of over seventy pages titled, 'SY FLIA: Project for Increasing Rice Production in 19__,' which gives the guiding principles and the steps to be

taken, as well as page after page of detail on the
area of land to go under different varieties of rice
in each village, calculated from the FLIA-wide target
as described in Chapter 5.

Minutes of (some) meetings are also kept in
careful detail. Every Monday morning a meeting is held
between the President, Manager, bureau chiefs, and heads
of HQ sections, at which the week's work is planned and
the previous week's work reviewed. This is highly
bureaucratised. Each Saturday every section office
and Field Station prepares a submission on its past and
planned week's work, and receives at the same time an
agenda for the Monday meetings. The minutes of the
meeting give one page per section and Field Station,
with a brief summary of its past week and a more
elaborate statement of what it is to do in the coming
week, divided into three or four main heads, each of
which is sub-divided into two or three more detailed
statements. These minutes are then distributed to every
member of the FLIA. However, at the daily meetings of
President, Manager and bureau chiefs, no minutes are
taken - and it appears the meetings are often cancelled.
At the once a month meeting of all staff, the President,
Manager and bureau chiefs lecture to the staff, not only
about FLIA activities but also about patriotism and the
achievements of the government of President Park. The
meeting concludes with a salute to the flag. There is
no discussion, no minutes are taken. If the President
is absent, the meeting is postponed till his return; it
is never taken by the Manager.

The main point then is that the extent of formalisation of procedures is high, and the amount and flow of
bureaucratically-processed information is large. What
is less clear is the use made of the information, and its
accuracy. We have seen that the main operational
activities - in particular the allocation of water and
the provision of agricultural extension - are not codified,
are not given much attention, do not call for much
information. In the huge body of codified procedures
and rules, there is almost no mention of 'farmers', no
mention at all of how the HNG are meant to operate nor
a job description for 'HNG Leader', nor, more surprisingly,
for the patroller.

One strongly suspects that much of the information
is collected, aggregated, and tabulated primarily for the
purpose of satisfying the government's inspectors or the
Ministry's performance targets, and that it has little
operational significance. This is reinforced by recalling
that statistics of area under different paddy varieties,
for example, are collected from HNG leaders, who are well
aware of the FLIA's interest in achieving its own targets
and who have nothing to lose by over-reporting; and that
the FLIA staff (like other agricultural agents responsible

for achieving target HYV areas) in any case have a
strong independent incentive to show an HYV area close
to the target.   Indeed, Reed found from a survey of
twenty-two villages in one township that township
officials were reporting HYV areas on average 70 percent
or more higher than the village heads reported directly
to him. [6]   Or again in Reed's study, township officials
reported 100 percent achievement of targets for establishment of joint farms - most of which existed only on
paper. [7]   Another example from SY FLIA: one Station
office in an area which grows a lot of vegetables has
on its wall a chart purporting to give height of vegetables
reached on such-and-such a date of 1979, compared with
the height reached on the same day of the previous year.
Naturally, the vegetables are always higher than the
previous year, and the information is bogus (if
impressive at first glance).   But perhaps most
revealing is the attitude of the staff to this and other
information.   Even the information on constant
measurements of the physical structure - such as the
length of branch canals - is often inconsistent from
one table to another, and the staff, in trying to
resolve the discrepancies for me often remarked, in the
dismissive words of one, 'These figures are all wrong'.
But recognition of this point does not lead them to try
to correct the figures, for correct figures are not
really necessary, it is enough to have some figures to
show.   No government inspector (the argument perhaps
runs) is going to know the difference.

WORK, LEISURE AND COMMUNITY

If the bogus quality of much of the information and
the absence of information on several key operational
parameters belies the general impression of efficiency
and control, so too does the work behaviour of the staff.
Over the year the work load fluctuates with the season,
each HQ section having one or two fairly short peak
periods in the year.   For the rest of the year the rhythm
is slow.   A leisurely read of the newspaper is the first
item of the day for all except the most junior, and the
newspaper will be returned to several times during the
course of the day. (Since the press is government-cont-
rolled, the government may by no means oppose careful
newspaper reading during office hours.)   The lunch-hour
is normally extended by half an hour to an hour.   By 4
to 4.30 pm half to two thirds of the HQ staff will be
away from the building, some of them on business.   The
office shuts officially at 6 pm and opens at 9 am.
The higher the position, the less work is done.
The great bulk of the work is done by the junior staff
at the far end of each section block of desks.   Their
desks display files and papers, neatly

stacked, while the desks of the section heads may have
one or two documents on them, and the bureau chiefs'
desks are completely clear. The section and bureau
chiefs spend a majority of their time in the office
chatting to each other or to an immediate subordinate;
or re-reading the newspaper; or looking out of the
window; or sleeping (the high-backed swivel armchairs
are especially useful in providing good head support and
for signalling, when swivelled away from the rest of the
office, that the occupant is not to be disturbed).
From time to time a clerk brings them something to sign.
They may glance through it before putting their
signature stamp to it.   The bureau chiefs give not even
a pretence of conscientious devotion to the job. [8]
    The staff, especially but by no means only the
senior-most, articulate strong feelings of SY FLIA as a
community. The relationships between staff are, in the
words of a grade 4, 'close and thick', and the image of
a big family is sometimes invoked to convey the notion
of a community of feeling. The staff are almost all
natives of the area within or adjacent to SY's
jurisdiction; many went to school together; many
travel to and from work together; those who live close
to others see them after work for drinking and eating;
it is expected that when a man's son gets married his
work colleagues will be invited to the wedding.   There
are sports competitions between the sections and Station
offices (mainly netball), and between the FLIA's team and
other government agencies like the ORD and the NACF;
impressive gold-plated figurines in athletic pose are
the trophies - one such currently dominates the wall by
the Land Development bureau, whose team came third in
the intra-FLIA netball competition.   (The headquarters'
town, population 60,000, has literally dozens of shops
specialising in trophies, certificates and other
symbols of competitive success.) There are also
monthly air-raid drills, and meant-to-be-once-a-week but
in practice less frequent group exercise sessions in
which all staff must participate in coordinated muscle
stretching to a rhythm chanted in unison, before a leader.
Such occasions as these tend to reinforce the sense of
groupness.   The frequent award to the FLIA of certificates
of outstanding achievement by the Minister of Agriculture
or the provincial governor may have the same effect. [9]
The framed certificates are arranged in a long row along
the wall of the Assembly Room.
    In interpersonal relations there is a blend of
formality, deference to rank, respect to age, on the one
hand, and an easy informality, a recognition of the
underlying equality of condition, on the other.   In the
morning staff will greet more senior staff with a bow
of the head, which will be reciprocated. Terms of public
address in the office almost always include the person's

position and surname: 'Clerk Kim', the chief of the
Administrative bureau addresses a junior employee, 'would
you mind ....', and Clerk Kim replies, 'Bureau Chief Park,
... '.   And the same applies to people of equal rank,
in public contexts.   At lunch time those who have
brought lunch boxes sit in a cluster at one of the blocks
of desks and eat together, from bureau chief down to
temporary employee.   In the mess room where lunches are
sold (subsidised handsomely by the FLIA) bureau and
section chiefs mix readily with whoever is there; not
uncommonly one or two will be seated in a foursome with
grade 5ers or employees. Their dress differs not at all
from that of junior staff (only the President sometimes
wears a suit, generally without tie).   At the same time,
of course, the symbols of hierarchy in the office layout
and furnishings are, as we have seen, sharply defined.
    This blend of two apparently opposing principles
is identified by Brandt as the key to social organisation
in the South Korean village he studied, and by implication,
Korean society more generally.   'I am postulating that
two distinct ethical systems affect ordinary, everyday
behaviour. One is formal and explicit. It is largely
lineage oriented and embodies a clearly structured
hierarchical system of rank and authority that is
closely linked with Korean aristocratic traditions, but
that has a pervasive effect on village life as well,
particularly with regard to kinship relations, personal
status, and ceremonial activity. On the other hand,
what I have called the egalitarian community ethic is
informal and has no codified set of moral principles,
although many aspects of it are expressed in proverbs
and homely aphorisms. Important values are mutual
assistance and cooperation among neighbours, hospitality,
generosity, and tolerance in dealing with both kin and
nonkin' (1971 , p. 25).   In the FLIA the bureaucratic
structure in a sense takes the place of lineage organisation in providing a sharply defined hierarchy of rank
and authority; but its expression in social interaction
is muted by the informal egalitarian ethic.
    How aggrieved, if at all, junior staff of the FLIA
feel at their subordinate position is difficult for an
outsider to know.   One factor which would tend to inhibit
such feelings is that the senior staff tend also to be
the oldest, because of the policy of recruiting to senior
positions by internal promotion. Confucian culture makes
a central virtue of respect for age, which is, in a sense,
a form of respect based on recognition of equality of
condition - for the young too will get old and receive the
same respect. To the extent that respect for age overlaps
with deference to rank, therefore, deference to rank may
not be felt as subordinating oneself.   Further the
frequent personal contact between ranks allows the hierarchy to be

exercised through paternalism in personal relations
rather than through abstract codifications and rules, and
this promotes vertical identification rather than
vertical opposition.   On the other hand, some young staff
did hint that they felt their seniors were excessively
conservative and uninterested in new ways of doing things,
and therefore unwilling to listen to their ideas with
the attention those ideas deserved; they felt
frustrated.   This however does little to impair the
effectiveness of the above features in overcoming the
differentiation which a bureaucratic hierarchy engenders,
by promoting a vertical and collective identification
by the lower ranks.

CONCLUSION

       One's first impression of SY FLIA is of
organisation charts, maps, rules, documents, records,
data, summary booklets, plans of action: of an
organisation in orderly control of its staff and
environment - highly 'bureaucratised', in short.   One's
second impression is of an easy, relaxed work rhythm,
shaped by a strongly symbolised work hierarchy.   Only
later does one discover that the high degree of
bureaucratisation applies only to those areas or sectors
of activities which are directly controlled by, subject
to scrutiny by, government.   These have to do primarily
with the organisation's income and expenditure, with
its staffing, and with communications between its
sections and between it and government.   On the other
hand, the activities which provide the FLIA's rationale -
delivering water, providing agricultural guidance, and
maintaining the structures - are much less subject to
scrutiny (excepting expenditure on maintenance), and
the farmers have no alternative channels through which
they might bring poor staff performance in these
activities to the attention of government.   FLIA
officials (as other public officials) are accountable
only to higher authorities for their performance, not
to the farmers.   Consequently, I argue, not only are the
main functions not codified (one small illustration
being the absence of job descriptions for the patrollers
and for HNG leaders, in contrast to the elaborate job
descriptions for graded staff), but little care and
attention is in fact given to these activities - though
more to maintenance and less to canal operation and
agricultural guidance.
       How common are the patterns reported here in the
South Korean public bureaucracy at large - especially
those patterns which suggest a lack of diligence,
conscientiousness, industriousness, a lack of concern for
the principal tasks of the organisation - must remain an
open question.   One would expect a relaxed work rhythm,

a leisurely life for the senior managers, a disinclination
to be concerned about what will not be monitored by a
superordinate office, to be more pronounced in
organisations like the FLIAs, which have to deal with
stable, slowly changing conditions, than in organisations
which have to face new and unfamiliar ones.   On the
other hand, the same approximately inverse correlation
between rank and work effort has been observed (casually)
in central government ministries in Seoul below the
topmost levels, which suggests that it may not be limited
to small, local parastatals. At any rate, we can conclude
with a caution about accepting uncritically an assumption
that the extraordinary efficiency of the whole public
bureaucracy has been a major element in South Korea's
development, a point to which we return in Chapter 8.
Meantime, we shall look at attempts by central
government to improve the FLIAs' performance, and draw
some wider comparisons between South Korea's
irrigation organisation and that of other countries.

NOTES

1. In national parastatals, like the Agricultural
Development Corporation, the President is appointed by
President Park.
2. The situation is somewhat more complex.
Employees are divided into three categories, typified
by 'driver', 'pump attendant', and 'typist'. Each
has a separate scale, the former highest, the latter
lowest. After 6 years, the salaries in the categories
are, respectively, 90,000 won a month, 72,500, and
50,000. Those in the 'typist' category are normally
young unmarried women. Their service increments stop
after six years, the other two categories stop after
ten years.   There are few employees in the 'typist'
category.
3. If they have to retire because of injury, they
get twelve months' salary plus the normal retirement
bonus.
4.   The formula is: number of years' service x
1.5 x monthly salary at retirement.
5. Acqua 1974, p. 50.
6. Reed 1979, p. 98, n. 27.
7. See Chapter 5, p.100,and Reed 1979, p. 205.

8. This generalisation, that workload is inversely
proportional to work, has been reported to me by others
from experience with central government ministries; however, at the very top levels, the relationship reverses
itself sharply, and workloads are typically immense.
This and the related observations about work performance
may surprise, given South Korea's phenomenal export success
and the important role of government in it. Let me make
it clear that my period of observation was June, July and
August, though I do not think that except for short
seasonal peaks the rest of the year is much different.
Secondly, it may be worth giving a couple of illustrations
from other contexts, by other observers, of the lack,
rather than the strength, of diligent, conscientious work.
Both illustrate a tendency to aim at rapid 'completion' of
a job, perhaps in line with targets, at the expense of
quality; a tendency related to what local officials have
in mind when they criticise the central government's
'showbusiness' or 'credit' policy. A UNDP/FAO report on
the upland development and watershed management project
observes, 'The quality of work /for the project/,
especially construction work, required constant supervision. The tendency to do a job quickly no matter how
well, as long as it looked satisfactory, could be observed
in all /17 / villages (1974, p. 256, emphasis added).
Secondly, Reed reports that in one of his case study
villages, 'rapid and shoddy work' made a fresh drinking
water supply system useless (1979, p. 94, n. 4).
9. One such certificate reads,

'A CERTIFICATE OF MERIT
From Minister of Agriculture   To SY FLIA 12.4.68

1st PRIZE

SY FLIA has the best rice yield amongst FLIAs in
the whole country. This is the result of all SY
staff working to do their best to guide farmers
and improve agricultural techniques.'

Another reads,

'LETTER OF APPRECIATION
From Head of X Province   To SY FLIA 19.7.1965

SY FLIA devoted itself to overcoming the severe
drought we have had this year, and cooperated well
with the government's policy for the emergency
period. As a result, SY area achieved high yields,
development of farmland, and improved farmers'
welfare. '

7
Irrigation Reform
and the Comparative Study
of Irrigation Organisation

One can distinguish two efforts at reform which have affected irrigation administration in the past decade, the first an extension of the New Community (Saemaul) Movement to the government bureaucracy generally, the second more recent and specific to irrigation.

NEW COMMUNITY MOVEMENT REFORM

For some years there has been concern in upper levels of government to make the government bureaucracy, and especially its rural side, less oriented towards enforcing the letter of bureaucratic regulations and self-profit, less oriented towards control and maintenance of the status quo, and more like an action-oriented instrument of social improvement. The latter might go with high levels of government control, as at present, but in a different form. An attempt has therefore been made to extend the spirit of the New Community Movement (NCM hereafter) into the government bureaucracy itself. At SY FLIA, the grade 2 staff and above have attended courses in 'spiritual education' (ideological training) at the national NCM training college, in place of vocational training given to grade 3 and below. And four times a year (since 1975) a set of lengthy questionnaires, called New Community reports, have to be filled in and sent via the provincial administration to the national head-quarters of the NCM, in the Blue House, office of President Park.

The Administrative staff complain about the laboriousness of the process. The questionnaire has a lot of words written in unfamiliar Chinese characters, and has first to be copied into Korean characters, all twelve pages, then sent to each section and Field Station head. The Administration staff have to draw up targets for each section and Station head to aim at, and coordinate the FLIA's overall plan. They then collate the replies, make them consistent with the overall plan, send the final document to the President for approval, then

onto the provincial government's special NCM office,
from where it goes on to the capital. The work is
claimed to be done in the name of the 'SY FLIA's New
Community Movement Committee', but in fact the committee
has no separate existence from the normal administrative
process.

The main headings on the questionnaire are:

1. Officers' ethics
2. Strengthening training
3. Devotion to the service of farmers
4. Staff's fulfilment of responsibilities and duties.

Some of the specific items under 1 and 2, on which
each section or Station head is asked to report progress
in the previous three months and plans for the next three,
are:

* Training, seminars, lectures on NCM
  - Overall, the FLIA plans to train 163 people for
    five months
* Keeping the environment clean
* Making a 'model' Field Station (for Field Station
  heads)
  - Yushin service system
  - Management system
  - Land consolidation & modernisation
  - Maintenance of all facilities
  - Increasing rights & freedoms of members
* Improving weaknesses in management
* Commendation of individual staff members in spirit
  of the NCM
  - Plan for ten people to be given awards by FLIA
    President
* Public relations activity on behalf of NCM
* Inspection and evaluation of above activities

Under heading 4, staff who have committed misdemean-
ours or received special awards are to be mentioned.
Otherwise however, the NCM reports are not seen as
reports on individuals, but on sections of organisations.
We have already considered heading 3 in the previous
chapter.

In addition to all this, each staff member is
required to sign a declaration of intent to apply the
NCM principles in his work, with each questionnaire.
The document bearing the signature stamps of all staff
members is forwarded to the provincial administration,
along with the FLIA's report.

It is of course difficult to evaluate the impact of
these procedures on staff work performance. I got the
impression that the administrators and especially the
section heads considered them a huge chore, which had,

however, to be diligently performed so as to make a good impression, because the government was obviously putting a lot of weight on the programme. It is quite possible however that the periodic raising in consciousness of their wider duties and responsibilities made some improvement in the care and consideration they brought to their work, especially in dealings with farmers.

But the effects, good or bad, are likely to be small besides those of a reform of irrigation which is planned to be introduced in the 1980 irrigation season.

THE PROPOSED FLIA REFORM

Despite the extensive powers of government over the FLIAs, the Ministry has not been able to stop several adverse trends:

1. A deteriorating balance between income and expenditure, resulting in a reduction in the relative size of each FLIA's savings fund, and an increased dependence on borrowing. The government gives cheap long term loans for maintenance and repair, but the loans cover only 70 percent of the total cost; and in practice relatively little money is available to the FLIAs under this heading. If money has to be borrowed for maintenance and repairs on a long term basis, much of it has therefore to be borrowed at the ordinary high rate of interest. More importantly, however, many FLIAs are now in a situation where much of the revenue from water charges (which accrues in a short period after the paddy harvest) goes to pay off the previous year's debts and interest, with the result that the FLIA again runs into debt later in the year and has to borrow short term at high interest to maintain its operations.

2. A relative decline in water charges: average charges have declined from 5.8 percent of average rice yield in 1966 (18.8 kgs. compared to 323 kgs. of rice per 0.1 hectare), to 3.7 percent in 1977 (18.5 kgs. out of 494).

3. An increase in the relative weight of administrative expenses: general administrative expenses (including salaries) now account for 25 percent of total (non-capital) expenditure on average; but 55 percent of the FLIAs spend more than 30 percent for this purpose.

4. A decrease in the relative weight of maintenance expenditure, while the number of facilities to be maintained increases: in the sixteen years between 1958 and 1973, total administrative ex-

penses were more than 75 percent of maintenance
and rehabilitation expenses in all years but one,
and greater than 100 percent in six years.
Maintenance expenditure now accounts for 36 percent of total expenditure on average, but the
government estimates it should be at least 40
percent, and only half the FLIAs reach this
level.

The Ministry of Agriculture believes the reasons
for these trends lie in the incentive structure facing
FLIA staff. As stated in the Ministry's booklet on the
reform and its rationale, the staff have 'lost the will
to modernise facilities, increase savings, increase
financial independence'. There is also the problem
that the farmers 'want to rely on government loans for
maintenance expenses, and want water charges to decrease
year by year' (Ministry of Agriculture, FLIA Management
Bureau, 1978, pp.7,9). The proposed reform, however, is
directed at the incentives and attitudes of staff, not
at the attitudes of farmers.

The reform aims to secure the compliance of FLIA
staff in solving these problems by making their salaries
dependent in part on their compliance. The FLIAs are to
be divided into three grades, A, B and C. This in fact
reintroduces a three grade classification in use until
the early 1970s. But whereas the old classification was
based simply on irrigated area, so that staff in bigger
FLIAs got higher salaries than those in smaller, the new
classification relates salary to the attainment of
certain levels of performance. There are basically two
criteria of classification; (1) the adequacy of the
physical structures, and of water supply throughout the
command area; and (2) the adequacy of the FLIA's own
financial reserves, which is the inverse of its need to
borrow for expenditure on other than major construction.
'A' FLIAs must have a savings fund of at lease 85 percent of annual current expenditure; 'B', 80 percent; 'C',
the rest. (Average size today is only 51 percent.) The
ranking of all 122 FLIAs will be done by the staff of the
Ministry's FLIA Management bureau. (These criteria are
somewhat similar to those used by the NCM to rank villages
into 'basic', 'self-helping', and 'independent', as
described in Chapter 5.)

'C' FLIAs will continue on the present salary scale;
'B' FLIAs will get salaries 15 percent higher; 'A's will
get another 15 percent on top of that. With this change
the staff of 'A' FLIAs will receive salaries almost as
high as the staff of the prestigious Agricultural Development Corporation (a national parastatal), and considerably higher than central government employees of equiv-

alent rank. At present, as we have seen, all FLIA staff
in South Korea of the same grade and length of service
are paid the same (though much use has been made of non-
pecuniary awards for FLIAs which get higher average rice
yields, or successfully help farmers fight a pest outbreak, or protect farmers against a drought, in the form
of display certificates signed by the provincial govern-
or, or the Minister of Agriculture, or by the President
of South Korea himself, as we noted earlier). The
Ministry firmly believes that the uniformity of salary
has sapped motivation amongst the FLIA staff (and
presumably that non-pecuniary incentives have not been
very effective).

It is expected that for the first few years at
least, very few of the FLIAs will make the 'A' grade
(though in principle there is no limit to the number
of FLIAs which can be so classified). To give a more
immediate incentive for improvement, there is another
component in the reform. All government employees in
South Korea get a 'bonus' of 400 percent of their monthly
salary each year automatically; as do FLIA staff. On top
of this regular bonus, the reform proposes an 'incentive
bonus' for FLIAs. Each year all the FLIAs will be
assessed against several performance indicators, and the
progress of each since the previous year measured. The
indicators are these:

- actual staff in relation to authorised staff
  (authorised according to the scale which links
  number of staff with size of command area):
  roughly speaking, the lower the better;
- the weight of general administrative expenses
  in total expenditure: the lower the better;
- the weight of the repair and maintenance expenses
  in total expenditure: the bigger the better;
- the size of the depreciation fund in relation to
  total expenditure: the bigger the better;
- the size of 'other savings' in relation to total
  expenditure: the bigger the better;
- the amount of interest paid as a proportion of
  total expenditure: the lower the better.

Whereas the A,B,C classification depends on level,
the incentive bonus depends on change since the previous
year. Those who do best will get another 100 percent of
monthly salary as an incentive bonus for that year; those
who do next best, 75 percent; next best again, 50 percent.
There is no fixed number of FLIAs which can receive
any of these bonuses; that is decided year by year by the
Ministry, which also - it is important to note - decides
year by year (presumably in advance) what weighting to
give each of the indicators, depending on what problems

it thinks most pressing. The instrument, then, is
intended to be non-discretionary as between different
FLIAs (though room for favouritism comes with the need
for central government staff to make judgements of such
matters as 'standard of water distribution'); but it is
also highly flexible from year to year.

But the FLIAs do have general targets to guide them:
management expenses should not be more than 30 percent
of the total, maintenance should be at least 40 percent,
the savings fund should be at least 100 percent of
current expenditure, and the depreciation fund should
rise from 36 kgs. of rice per hectare to 150 kgs. by
1982. With these targets the FLIAs are given an idea of
what the Ministry considers good levels of performance.

Finally, the motivation problem will also be
tackled by improving and expanding the in-service training given to staff. Already in 1978 150 FLIA administrators and 350 technicians from across the country were
given training for periods of two and three weeks each
at the Agricultural Development Corporation's central
training college, as the start of a big expansion in
this type of training (but as noted earlier, the most
senior staff are to be given not vocational but leadership and political training at the national NCM college).
It is hoped that as well as improving the staffs'
ability to do their jobs, the education will also 'make
a closer relationship between staff and members', by
promoting a 'close and positive attitude' of staff towards farmers. Only to this minor degree does the
proposed reform talk about improving the connection
between staff and farmers.

It is to be noted that the reform proposes no
change in the farmers' role: they are not to have a say
in seasonal or long-term water or financial decisions,
nor in the selection of the President (and senior staff).
An agricultural economist who recently wrote a cost-
benefit report on land development projects in South
Korea inserted into his concluding remarks the suggestion
that farmers should be given a greater role in the
selection of their FLIA's president, but deleted the
passage on government instructions.

FLIA STAFF'S REACTION TO THE REFORM

At SY FLIA reaction to the proposed reform has
been unenthusiastic, even hostile. One senior staffer
called it 'an interruption and a worry'. The reaction
is based on five main grounds: (1) The staff dislike
the attempt to use income as an incentive. As several
said, they already work at the maximum anyway, so it
cannot lead to increased effort. One man commented,
'It is a mean affair, because the staff of FLIAs every-

where do the same work, put in the same effort, regardless of whether the FLIA is A, B, or C'. (2) In fact, they went on to say, the new scheme discriminates against new FLIAs which have to spend relatively large amounts on getting the 'bugs' out of the technology at the beginning, and can devote less income to the savings fund - on which, as they see it, the A,B,C, ranking basically depends (since it is readily quantifiable, while 'adequacy of physical structures', 'adequacy of water distribution' are not). (3)'No FLIA', said a senior man, 'wants the goal of complete financial independence from the government' - not least because the rate of interest on loans is lower than the rate of inflation, so the FLIA managers want to borrow rather than save. (4) The new measures will prompt increases in water charges, especially in the case of a FLIA trying to get into the 'A' rank, and there is a general feeling at SY FLIA that current charges should not be increased further because the farmers could not afford to pay more. (5) The staff see it as an attempt by the central government to push them around. 'It is central government's plan', said one, 'and does not give enough consideration to the staff of the FLIA'. Greater financial independence will not, they think, lead to less overall government control.

Little is known about the perceptions of staff in parastatals and field agencies towards the central government in South Korea, and it may perhaps seem surprising that the criticism of the central government reform was as strong and as outspoken. It is also worth noting the feeling amongst the staff at SY FLIA of common interest with staff of 'FLIAs in general' (and especially new FLIAs), even though there is no formal national association of FLIA staff through which a sense of corporateness might be fostered, and even though the staff at each FLIA tend to stay with that FLIA for life, rather than move from one FLIA to another. And finally, it is worth noting that the salient point for discussion amongst staff was not so much how much better off they would be if they made 'A' grade, but whether they would have to increase water charges - there was a distinct reluctance to do so. This suggests that although the formal mechanisms of accountability of staff to farmers are extremely weak, there is nevertheless a diffuse sense of what 'the farmers' as a body will tolerate and what they will not. At least this seems to be the implication. Yet one would like to know more about a response that apparently places more weight on the interests of the clients than on their own interest in higher salaries, an apparent renunciation of sectional interest in favour of the wider interest of the less powerful. One would also like to know more about the circumstances and contexts in which FLIA staff see themselves as agents of the central government in relations with farmers.

If the reaction of SY staff is at all typical, the effectiveness of the reform in terms of its intended objectives is less than certain. This adds to the interest of following-up the implementation of the reform, as a case study in the use of one major type of policy instrument. At present, the FLIAs are controlled by instruments of discretionary command, and such instruments are widely used throughout the South Korean economy, as we have seen. The FLIA reform proposes to rely more heavily on instruments to manipulate the organisation's field of choice, such that compliance carries its own reward, rather than on command; and on manipulation in a relatively non-discretionary way. As the South Korean economy becomes more complex one can expect a general trend away from policy instruments of discretionary command towards those of non-discretionary manipulation. But suppose the FLIAs are slow to respond. At what point and how will even stronger instruments, whether of discretionary manipulation of the field of choice or of discretionary command, be introduced? To answer this one would need to know more than we know at present about why the existing mechanisms of control, through the President and the budget, have not been more effective means of reversing the trends.

COMPARISON WITH TAIWAN

The similarities and differences in irrigation organisation of South Korea and Taiwan invite systematic study. The two countries have a similar agriculture, of small-scale rice producers embraced by a powerful state. Both countries have watershed-defined irrigation parastatals, which still owe much to their common origins in Japan's Irrigation Associations. But one of the distinguishing features of Taiwan's Irrigation Associations has been a commitment to the needs of the farmers, something which the evidence of this study suggests is much weaker in South Korea; and this difference, with its widely ramifying manifestations, seems to rule out talk of an 'East Asian' model of (non-socialist) irrigation organisation, with South Korea put together with Taiwan or Japan.

Yet even this conclusion cannot be taken without question. For there are no detailed interpretive studies (in English) against which the Taiwanese side of the comparison may be gauged - we have a few good accounts of the water allocation procedures of the Irrigation Associations, but scanty evidence on how decisions are actually made and implemented; we know that the Irrigation Associations have better defined mechanisms of liaison with farmers, better techniques of feedback

and response; but we do not know much about how these
are operated in practice. Furthermore, it may be that
the very high level of managerial control over water
which is possible in Taiwan exceeds what is economically
justified; the cost of maintaining that control potential
may be much higher than the gains which are reaped on
the infrequent occasions (perhaps in a once in four
years' drought) when the whole of the control potential
has to be brought into use. There is a good deal of
congratulatory literature on Taiwanese irrigation which
fails to raise these questions.

Moreover, the 1975 reform of Irrigation Associations
in Taiwan was towards a more centralised administration -
the twenty-four existing Irrigation Associations were
consolidated into sixteen, the locally elected Irrigation Association's Representative Assembly was abolished
(which happened in South Korea in 1961), the Irrigation
Association's Chairman and senior technical staff were
to be appointed by the head of the Department of Reconstruction upon the recommendation of the Provincial
(that is, all-Taiwan) Water Conservancy Bureau, and the
central government was to be given greater control of
the Association's financial affairs. This would seem
to be a step towards controlling the Irrigation Associations by techniques of discretionary command, in the
opposite direction to South Korea's proposed reform.
On the other hand, South Korea's FLIAs are very much
smaller in jurisdiction than Taiwan's Irrigation Associations, they are many more in total number, and the
difference in reform emphasis may reflect the fact that
it is much easier to control sixteen organisations by
discretionary command than 122.

But what makes the comparison between South Korea
and Taiwan both difficult and fruitful is that, while
many features of agriculture, political regime, and
culture are similar, there is much greater concern for
maximising water productivity and efficiency in Taiwan.
This reflects, in part, the climatic difference which
permits two or more irrigated crops a year in Taiwan
and only one in South Korea; and perhaps also a greater
commitment by government to providing service to the
farmers, for reasons having more to do with political
legitimacy than economic optima. But in South Korea
the cost of developing new water sources and irrigated
land has been rising rapidly in the past decade
(especially as expansion has tended to be concentrated
on tide-land reclamation); and new higher yielding
varieties suitable for South Korea's climate have
become available since the early 1970s. For both
reasons the value on water use efficiency is rising in
relation to the cost of providing this efficiency. And
since the early 1970s the government has become more

concerned to be seen to be 'pro rural'. The new
irrigation reform, however, does little to improve <u>main</u>
system operation; for example, no suggestion has been
made for introducing rotational delivery to sub-units
of the command areas, not even on a pilot project basis,
despite the evidence from Taiwan (and some from experiments in South Korea) of very large gains in water use
efficiency. The possibilities are not even being discussed. One suspects that more is involved here than
a simple response to environmental pressures. As the
value on water efficiency increases in relation to the
costs of providing it, as the government becomes more
sensitive to the dangers of a severe drought for social
order and for the government's own legitimacy, the possibilities of improved main system operation will come
to be discussed and changes may be introduced, as they
were in Taiwan in the 1954-55 reform which introduced
rotational irrigation on a wide scale. But how long
this will take depends on, amongst other things, the
response of local FLIA staff. We have seen that the
incentives on them are to guard carefully those activities subject to scrutiny of government, and to pay
little attention to those activities not subject to
scrutiny. The present reform will not alter the concentration of attention away from water delivery and
agricultural guidance. A major new reform - or struggle
by central government to control its local agents - will
be needed.

On the other hand, the fact that water scarcity is
less of a problem in South Korea than in many other
countries means that the staff's lack of attention to
water scheduling matters less than it would elsewhere,
as also does the lack of an effective mechanism for
liaison between staff and farmers. In the South Korean
context, the chief concern the farmers would push if
they had more influence in the irrigation associations
would be administrative economy - they would want to
scrutinise the accounts. Officials' conduct would
therefore be more threatened, and they can argue against
democracy on the grounds that farmers would want penny-
pinching economies, and only far-sighted, technically
competent and responsible officials can properly judge
what types and levels of expenditure are really necessary. Where water use efficiency is at issue, however,
as it is in Taiwan and much of South and Southeast Asia,
the chances of reforms which permit farmer involvement
may be better, if government can be persuaded that such
involvement is the only way to get legitimate resolution
of (scarcity-induced) conflicts and hence amongst other
things, an effective way to protect its <u>workable</u> authority in the countryside.

The facts of water supply are only one reason why
there is little to be learnt from South Korea's irrig-

ation experience of direct relevance to countries of
South and Southeast Asia. There are also important
cultural differences - the pattern of authority relations
described earlier is strikingly different from that of
cultures where authority is expected to be - or often,
for effectiveness, needs to be - aloof and domineering;
people of Confucian culture more completely, and apparently genuinely, take on the goals of organisation as
their personal goals; the desire to be considered a
good member of the group is a more important motive for
action than in, say, India; and so on.

These points all suggest why caution is needed in
drawing conclusions about the desirability in South or
Southeast Asian contexts of the 'Irrigation Association'
type of organisation. There are specific technical and
organisational procedures which can be learned from
Taiwanese (but not South Korean) irrigation management
and which might be usefully introduced elsewhere, and
the elucidation of what these are would be eminently
valuable; but there can be no assumption that the same
benefits in terms of work orientation and organisational involvement of staff would follow.

The main general lesson about irrigation organisation from the present study, rather, is methodological.
I have emphasised throughout that irrigation organisation can be understood only partly as a response to
conditions of water and agriculture, and this holds
even where water scarcity is much more acute than in
South Korea. It is also shaped by wider institutions,
ways of doing things; and specifically by processes of
bureaucratisation and control in government administration, and by the procedures and mechanisms that work to
prevent or facilitate the articulation of the interests
of non-powerful groups and classes. Irrigation politics,
in the broad sense, condition the impact of irrigation
on production and employment. Yet the political dimen-
sion of irrigation performance has so far been almost
wholly ignored. For the future the interplay between
irrigation politics and economics deserves high priority
for explanatory research; and conversely research which
concentrates on the input-output relations between
irrigation, production and employment, treating the
administrative organisation as a black box, will miss
critical issues.

8
State Control
and Interpretations
of South Korean Development

Professional economists..., like members of
any tribe, operate within conceptual frame-
works of the kind which anthropologists call
'collective representations'.... In the
field of economic development, two mutually
exclusive sets of associated ideas are
often juxtaposed against each other: one
set consists of capitalism, free trade and
export promotion and the other, socialism
State intervention and import substitution.
In our view these collective representations
have done considerable damage to our understanding of the Korean phenomenon.
                    (Datta-Chaudhuri 1979, p. 53)

...the masses of Asia have come to believe
that free economy is rather a hindrance than
a help to development... (Park Chung Hee
1962, p. 205).

Let us return to those sharply contrasting and
passionately defended interpretations of South Korea's
development to which I referred at the start of this
essay.   It is clear that a study of the state in
action in one small corner of its domain cannot
support much by way of generalisation; but it can
help to qualify and amplify interpretations of the
large-scale trends current in the literature.
The great bulk of that literature comes out of
the theoretical tradition of neo-classical
economics.   Indeed, South Korea has a central place
in neo-classical thinking about development in
general, because it (as well as Taiwan) provides or
appears to provide the living example that the broad
neo-classical prescription for development is
empirically well grounded.   In large part as a

response to the congratulatory mode of the neo-classicals, there is a substantial denunciatory literature which denies the viability and progressiveness of South Korea's development, emphasising its dependence on external support and internal repression. [1]   We begin then, by briefly setting these interpretations of South Korea in the context of the wider development debate.

SOUTH KOREA IN THE DEVELOPMENT DEBATE

The import-substituting industrialisation strategies put forward in the 1950s were a response to the observed difficulties of earning adequate foreign exchange through agricultural exports and to the absence of industrial sectors capable of with-standing international competition in export markets. The theorists of import substitution talked of the need for a 'big (investment) push', for 'balanced growth' or 'unbalanced growth', with the implication of a substantial directive role for the state in the economy.   The investment pattern was not to be left to be revealed by the market; rather, market signals were to be deliberately 'distorted' by state inter-vention and sometimes even set aside, in the interests of explicitly defined national development objectives. Neo-classical economists found this broad approach thoroughly unsavoury.

By the mid 1960s, with import substituting industrialisation policies themselves seen to be highly problematic in application, the development debate tended to polarise.   On the one hand, there was a strong affirmation of the neo-classical route via labour-intensive manufactured exports in line with comparative advantage, with government inter-vention limited primarily to getting the prices right - either or both to ensure the conditions in which markets can work freely, or to use taxes, transfers and subsidies to produce the prices which would have happened if there had been no market 'distortions'.   On the other hand came an affirmation that the problems of import-substitution were less those of the strategy itself as of dependent capitalist development generally, and that the only viable development path was a socialist alternative involving a break from integration with the world economy.

In this context the South Korean case became a focus of debate.   The neo-classicals argued from the late 1960s that South Korea was proving that their prescription worked - not only could it

produce fast growth, but equitable growth as well.
Just as strongly, the radicals said South Korea was
a 'house built on sand'. Neither side, it seems to
me, is correct.

By 1980 it is reasonably clear that the South
Korean experience is not consistent with the
'impossibility'theorem of many dependency writers.
The gains and losses from foreign trade do not
follow simply from a country's central or peripheral
role in the world economy. While some countries
have indeed become trapped in the role of unprocessed
food and raw material exporters with little sign of
being able subsequently to build up a suitably
developed economic structure, foreign trade has in
some conditions undoubtedly provided the incentive
for the country to develop a more advanced structure.
South Korea shows that intensive use of resources
and rapid movement up the product cycle towards high
skill and high technology industries can be brought
about while maintaining relatively liberal trading
policies - with sufficient efficiency (in conventional economic terms) for the new industrial sectors
to be able to compete in international markets and
respond to international price signals, and with
strong and sustained increases in real wages for the
bulk of the labour force. We see now in South
Korea an economy with an inbuilt 'dynamism' - with a
capacity to sustain near full employment of labour
while heavily exposed to international competitive
pressures, which means it has enough economic
flexibility to respond to changing international
conditions and enough emerging technological
capability to withstand international competition.
Admittedly one cannot be sure as of 1980 how robust
this dynamism will be in the face of a continuing
world economic stagnation and the oil price rises of
the 1970s; but the balance of probability is
strongly in favour. The question about South Korea
is how it has acquired its inbuilt dynamism, when
many other Third World countries have not.

THE LIMITATIONS OF THE NEO-CLASSICAL INTERPRETATION

The neo-classical answer runs in terms of the
abilities of the people - a skilled, disciplined,
conscientous workforce - and good policies. Good
policies refer to 'almost free trade conditions for
exporters', 'free labour markets', and 'high interest
rates', which provided the conditions in which
private entrepreneurs produced labour-intensive growth.[2]
Other countries could (and should) create these same

conditions. The 'you-too-can-have-a-body-like-mine' optimism is explicit in Brown's exuberant statement that, 'The almost irresistable conclusion from Korean development experience is that with proper economic policies and a continuation of reasonable international aid levels most developing countries can achieve at least a 6 per cent annual growth rate, and many countries could sustain growth rates as high as 10 per cent' (1973, p. 265).
   This answer overlooks several key points. [3]

   (1) The international economy in the mid 1960s (when South Korea's manufactured export drive began) was in an expansionary phase, characterised in particular by two conditions whose combination was crucial for allowing the 'newly industrialising country' (NIC) phenomenon to take place: a ready supply of capital from industrialised countries to cheap labour sites, either as loans to domestic producers or as equity investment; and, as part of the increasing struggle for competitive advantage between the industrialised countries, relatively free access for cheap labour goods in selected categories to the vast markets of the United States and Japan. Increasingly through the 1970s this combination has ceased to exist, as import barriers have been erected in one industrial country after another in response to weakening home demand and rising unemployment. This alone must heavily qualify the relevance of the South Korean model for other countries today. [4]

   (2) South Korea was unusually well placed to take advantage of emerging opportunities for cheap labour manufactured exports. First, the ease of getting foreign aid and loans and the ease of entry into the American market were not unrelated to South Korea's geo-political significance to the United States in the struggle against 'Communism' (which also procured it extraordinarily high levels of military assistance). Its close trade and investment relations with Japan were not unrelated to its cultural affinities, geographical proximity, and history as Japan's colony. Second, by 1960, before the export boom began, South Korea had a relatively highly developed economic structure, including a sizable industrial sector (helped by import substitution policies) and a highly productive foodstuff-producing agriculture - an economic structure which was nationally owned and nationally operated. It had no large landed estates,

no aristocratic class based on landholding. It had an unusual degree of equality in land and industrial ownership. It also had no natural resource base from which exports might have been derived - which helps to explain why the emphasis fell so heavily and with so little internal opposition upon exports o f manufactures. Labour-intensive manufactures clearly can be a 'leading sector', in the sense that they create a mass demand for labour, for raw materials and other industrial goods, and so can stimulate the creation of other industries; whereas the production of many (but not all) agricultural goods and raw materials does not have this trans-forming potential. South Korea also had a relatively highly educated labour force; and an unusual degree of ideological homogeneity. Finally, its people had many years of experience under the Japanese of a 'hard', dictatorial, growth-oriented regime (but oriented towards the provisioning of the Japanese economy). These advantages (which Taiwan also shared) seem to call for substantial qualification to Little's statement that the success of South Korea, as well as Taiwan, Hong Kong and Singapore, is due 'scarcely at all to favourable circumstances or a good start' (1979, p. 4). They further reduce South Korea's relevance as a model for other countries.

(3) The South Korean state was able to concentrate the process of capital accumulation with-in Korea, with control remaining predominantly in Korean hands, and directed in a coherent manner at long-run, nationally-defined objectives. It did this not only by means of influencing prices, but also by extensive use of non-price instruments, including discretionary command, in a manner quite inconsistent with the neo-classical prescription. This role has been crucial in allowing South Korea and Taiwan to succeed in the NIC export strategy, where other countries have not. Their industrialisation has occurred not as a passive process of responding to market forces, but as a process tightly directed by the state.

(4) The country's population was sufficiently small for a relatively small volume of South Korean manufactured exports (compared to the world total) to exert so much demand for labour as to cause demand-induced increases in wages, and a far-reaching transformation of the structure of the economy.
In these conditions, the South Korean strategy

has indeed worked, and has resulted in a wide dispersal of the material benefits of growth. 'Trickle-down' has indeed occurred. Technological progress has been sufficiently rapid for the alternative of responding to competitive pressure by bearing down heavily on the cost of labour not to have been followed (the average real wage rate in manufacturing establishments employing more than 10 workers has been increasing at around 10 percent per year between 1962 and 1978).[5] If one distinguishes the effectiveness of a regime (defined in terms of its ability to promote 'modernisation') and its legitimacy (the belief that it has the right to exercise political authority), then the Park regime in South Korea has certainly gained some legitimacy amongst the population at large by its demonstrated ability to direct a growth process fast and egalitarian enough to bring significant material benefits to the bulk of the population. Long (1977) and others on the Left are much too simple in arguing that the survival of the regime is due largely to foreign assistance and internal repression - indeed, the fact of direct repression is itself a response to the success of the regime in diffusing economic and educational benefits widely, and the consequent desire of large sections of the population not to remain politically inert.

The question is why the power of the state has been used so as to promote, rather than impede, a viable and relatively egalitarian pattern of development, with production remaining predominantly in Korean hands. The contrast with, say, Brazil or Kenya is sharp. Yet this question, apparently so central, is one to which little research has been directed.

LEADERSHIP COMMITMENT TO GROWTH

To say that this 'progressive' (if also repressive) use of the state's power reflects the leadership's commitment to fast, nationally-controlled growth is a first step. [6] Undoubtedly the personal value hierarchy of President Park has been of some significance in explaining that commitment. In sharp contrast to his predecessor, Rhee Syng Man (who ruled from 1948 to 1960), Park reiterated again and again that the first task, before a liberal economy or polity could be constructed, was to eliminate starvation and despair - a condition which he himself, as farmer's son and country schoolteacher, had seen at close quarters. 'It is', he said in 1962,

'also an undeniable fact that the people in Asia
today fear starvation and poverty more than the
oppressive duties thrust upon them by totalitarianism
.... the masses of Asia have come to believe that
free economy is rather a hindrance than a help to
development.... the Asian peoples want to obtain
economic equality first, and build a more equable
political machinery afterwards' (1962, p. 204, 205).

Many political leaders around the world have,
of course, voiced similar sentiments. The commitment to translating this value hierarchy into action
has been stiffened in South Korea's case by the
mind-concentrating presence of a hostile, heavily
armed, rapidly industrialising, egalitarian North
Korea on South Korea's doorstep (Seoul is less than
three minutes by jet fighter from the border).
While most 'bureaucractic authoritarian' regimes
have had to invoke the threat from 'internal enemies'
to justify the curtailment of citizen participation,
South Korea (conversely for the North) had the advantage, so to speak, of a most tangible external
enemy, one which was seen by the leadership as a
threat not only to national security but to the very
existence of the 'free way of life'. The military
officers who took power in 1961 were acutely aware
that North Korea's industrialisation was proceeding
with extraordinary rapidity, and that with such an
economic base North Korea had a good chance of
winning a war if South Korea's powerful allies
hesitated to come to its aid. [7] The presence of
North Korea has served to discipline the leadership's
use of state power in the interests of a fast and
relatively egalitarian growth - for if disparities
became too great unrest might begin to be widely
voiced, sections of the population might begin to
compare the South unfavourably with the (imagined)
North (where many have close relatives), and
northern guerillas might find support in the
southern countryside.

The pressures for maintenance of a relatively
egalitarian income distribution (or for not taking
certain measures which would have worsened income
distribution) have probably come - it is difficult
to be certain - more from the President's Office,
the military, and the Korean Central Intelligence
Agency than from the economic ministries; it is the
former group which is more aware of the potential
for unrest if income disparities are allowed to
become too great. This may be why, when rural
unrest did begin to be widely expressed in the
late 1960s after several years of stringent terms

of trade for agriculture, the state acted swiftly to
bring up rural incomes (and also to exert tighter
control in the countryside through the Saemaul
Movement), even though this caused increases in
food prices and led to increases in wage costs which
weakened the competitiveness of Korean exports.
In the late 1970s the question of food prices is
again a major contest, with the economic ministries
wanting more food imports to keep down the cost of
labour, and the Agriculture Ministry and the President's office inclining towards less imports,
even at the expense of higher food prices and
higher labour costs, in the interests of keeping up
rural incomes so as both to reduce rural unrest and
to stem the flow of people to the cities.
        During the 1970s, as the goal of catching up
with North Korea's industrial capacity came within
reach, the target shifted more towards Japan: the
aim was to catch up with the admired, envied, and
disliked former colonial power. (Not until 1965
were diplomatic relations re-established with Japan
after the Second World War and then against much
popular opposition.) The fear of again being over-
whelmed by, made subordinate to Japan is a notable
reason why, from the beginning of the inflow of
foreign private capital in the mid 1960s, the
government has adopted a cautious, restrictive
policy towards direct foreign investment. Only
about 10 percent of total foreign capital inflow
over the past twenty years has been direct investment (much of that in one sector, electronics).
When the balance of payments became more favourable
in the late 1970s, there was strong pressure from
parts of the government to eliminate further foreign
investments. [8]   From the standpoint of neo-classical
economics, this restrictive attitude to international
capital makes little sense. The recipient of equity
investment has only to pay back out of realised
profits whereas the recipient of loans has to pay
back a fixed amount regardless of profits. But
loans are associated with less dilution of national
control of production.
        While the Japanese factor is undoubtedly
important in explaining this concern of the South
Korean leadership, its origins are much deeper. In
the nineteenth century the country was called the
Hermit Kingdom because of the Korean suspicion of
foreigners. The relatively autarchic development
strategy followed in North Korea owes much to this
suspicion, which can more readily be acted upon
than in the South because of the North's generous

supplies of natural resources.   It is striking that
in his 1979 book, <u>Korea Reborn: A Model for
Development</u>, Park gave cardinal importance to the
concept of <u>jaju</u> - 'being master in one's own house',
a concept with more than a passing resemblance to
<u>juche</u>, the idea of 'self-reliance' which has guided
North Korea's development strategy. [9]   The North
Korean development 'model' and the South Korean
'model' are not in fact as fundamentally contrasting
as most writers on the Right and on the Left assume.

The fact that in South Korea entrepreneurship
and management has been predominantly in Korean
hands has had a very important consequence: compared
to many Third World countries where foreign capital
has been welcomed with open arms, there has not been
a clear separation between an 'international bourgeoisie' of Koreans employed by multi-national firms,
and a 'national bourgeoisie'. The contrast with
Brazil or Kenya is again striking. In this respect,
the dynamics of South Korean development have been
significantly different from the typical case of
peripheral capitalist development assumed by dependency theory. [10]   In particular, the leadership
commitment to a <u>nationally</u> defined development
strategy has been easier to maintain and implement
than otherwise. And that matters, because while
from the perspective of multi-national firms it
does not much matter whether it is Korean levels of
technology which are improved or someone else's, it
makes a great deal of difference to the people of
Korea - including the workers - that technology
levels <u>in Korea</u> should be improved.

'ONE CAPITAL'

The restrictive policy towards foreign direct
investment has meant that vis-a-vis multi-national
capital the South Korean state has had a notable
degree of autonomy of action.   So too with
national capital. Internationally, it is true,
South Korean firms behave as if they were independent
agents, and this seems to justify the neo-classical
focus on relations between 'the economy' and the
outside world, via such variables as exchange rates.
When one investigates the way decision-making works,
however, a different interpretation is suggested. [11]
The pressures of the international market are
allowed to bear down on South Korean firms, as they
do on a multi-national company. But within South
Korea, as within a multi-national, relations between
the components are not regulated simply according to

market forces; the element of administrative
allocation is large.   There is indeed a large
private sector, and big business is in a certain
sense powerful.   But power is not an undifferentiated
concept.   Even more than in Japan, individual South
Korean firms, especially the big emerging multi-
nationals, can be understood not as independent units
of capital but as 'one capital', as parts of a wider
unit with each part having restricted choices about
domestic and foreign involvement.   The agency which
orchestrates the parts, which forces individual
capitalists to take a long-term view and mediates
between the South Korean social unit and the outside,
is the state.   In this sense big South Korean firms
are not as powerful as one would expect from other
economies; they have only weak means of asserting
their individual interests against the collective
interests of South Korean capital.

     In other words, one of the key questions about
South Korean development concerns the conditions
which have made or encouraged the owners and
managers of (big) private capital to use their
control over resources in a way which is consistent
(on the whole) with a national interest - as distinct
from a way which maximizes their own individual
short-term profits (which may include selling out to
a multi-national, or speculating in domestic real
estate, for example).   The answer relates to the
role of the state.   While its directive role in the
economy has been important since the early 1960s,
it has been especially dominant since the early 1970s
in restructuring the economy towards heavy and
chemical industries - in the second half of the 1970s
the state has ensured that fully 75-80 percent of new
equipment investment of major private manufacturing
enterprises has gone to heavy and chemical industry,
leaving only 20-25 percent for light industry, [12]
on the model of the Japanese push into these industries in the 1950s.

     The details of how the state has orchestrated
the activities of the private industrial sector are
beyond the scope of this essay, and in any case have
been explored in the recent study by Jones and Sa-
Kong (1978).   Suffice it to say that the key instrument of discretionary control has been the granting
or withholding of subsidized credit through the
government-monopolised banking sector; and a second
important instrument has been the tax audit.   With
tight discretionary control over investment and
export decisions able to be exerted via the capital
market, the government could afford to establish a

set of relatively liberal foreign trading policies.[13]
The neo-classical focus on the link between trading
policies and growth has thus been misleading, for it
has obscured the significance of capital market
controls as means of state direction of economic
activity.   Or to put the point more generally, the
neo-classical argument that the liberalisation of
trade caused (was the major cause of) rapid
economic growth in South Korea overlooks the fact
that the liberalisation of trade was itself
facilitated by conditions conducive to rapid - and
nationally-oriented - growth, such as state direction
of the capital market.

'ONE FARM'

In this essay we have seen the government's directing
role primarily in the countryside.   Pricing policies
have certainly been important in helping to bring
about the big increases in rural living standards
(especially the rice producer subsidies in the 1970s)
and in inducing adoption of HYVs. But the earlier
discussion (Chapter 5) of the <u>Saemaul</u> Movement, the
HYV programme, the fertiliser programme, the pest
control programme, provides many illustrations of
the importance of exhortation, discretionary bargaining, deception, outright coercion, mobilisation of
peer group pressure, for achieving objectives
imposed from above.   These are not the methods
prescribed in the rural development textbooks of the
West.
      Indeed, as suggested earlier, it makes nearly
as much sense to describe South Korean agriculture
as 'one farm' as to describe it as 'small-scale
family farming', because the area of farmers' free
decision-making is tightly constrained by the
monopoly and monopsony power of the state.   There
is a parallel to be drawn between the structural
position of South Korean farmers in relation to
officials and that of tenants in relation to landlords in parts of South Asia.   The latter are
commonly involved in multistranded relationships with
a single landlord, who supplies each tenant not only
with land but also with production credit, some
material inputs, a house, consumption loans, and
employment on his self-operated land;   and in
addition the landlord may market much of the tenant's
own share of the output.   This system of interlinked
markets and resource domains, going with the absence
of arms-length trading, allows the landowner greater
control over resources and appropriation of a greater

share of the economic surplus; [14] and makes the
overt expression of discontent by the subordinate
party more difficult. The mechanism of control in
the South Korean case is rather similar and is
similarly used to avert expressions of discontent -
though here the similarity ends, for by and large
the targets and orders which local officials use
their power to implement are more closely related
to improvements in mass welfare than are those of
South Asian landlords, and farmers know that local
officials are under heavy pressure from above
rather than being themselves the source of coercion.

Yet this essay cannot claim to have got further
than the few other studies of rural policy implementation inlaying bare the processes by which the more
discretionary and punitive instruments are used -
and by which those at whom they are directed attempt
to evade or lessen their force. It is clear that
government officials use the multiplex ways in which
farmers depend on local government (or parastatal)
offices and agencies for inputs (notably credit,
fertiliser, seeds, insecticides) as a means for
securing their compliance to specific orders or
targets. It is likely that this happens partly via
informal social relations between employees in the
various local government institutions. Whether the
membrane of local government institutions is so thin
that an agricultural extension officer, himself under
pressure to achieve a certain set of targets, might
be able to reach into, for example, the school
system and threaten a child's progress if the
father's compliance on HYVs is not forthcoming,is a
question to which we do not know the answer. But
within the set of agricultural input and marketing
agencies, notably the ORD and the NACF, and probably
the Saemaul Movement as well, such permeability does
exist and is used to secure compliance.

The 'one farm' and 'one capital' image is to be
contrasted with the image presented by neo-classical
economics, of government intervention almost wholly
through policies on incentives. Thus Hong,
'Planning in Korea implied setting up physical
targets and marshalling various tax-subsidy measures
to achieve these objectives' (1980, p. 34).
Westphal, in a long and careful analysis of South
Korea's industrial development, says virtually
nothing about discretionary command. He acknowledges
in passing, at the end, that 'Korea has a strong
government motivated and able to impose far-reaching
economic policies' (1978, p. 375), but as examples
gives devaluations, tax measures, and keeping labour

markets free, all non-discretionary instruments.
He mentions the export targeting system as an
example of a non-price intervention complementary
to incentive policies; and goes on, 'One
important function filled by the export targeting
system was to keep the government well informed
regarding export performance so that timely changes
could be made in <u>incentives</u>, often including <u>ad
hoc assistance</u> to individual exporters' (p. 376 ,
<u>emphasis added</u>).   Little says with characteristic
succinctness, 'Planning ... and the public sector,
have not, in my opinion, played key roles' (1979,
p. 36).

THE POLITICAL REGIME

The political regime which has carried out the
state's directing, coercing, encouraging role has
been variously described as 'fascist', 'bureaucratic
authoritarian', a 'repressive military dictatorship',
and 'fascade democracy'. 'Authoritarian' is certainly appropriate, if used in the ordinary sense of a
regime in which obedience to authority is given much
more weight than individual liberties and in which
control over the exercise of that authority is weak.
Power is concentrated strongly in the executive;
the legislature, judiciary, and local/regional units
have little autonomy.   Electoral competition is very
restricted, freedom of interest associations likewise,
and use of repression a normal technique of rule.
But 'fascist' is misleading, for mass mobilisation,
a mass political party to link state and civil
society, are lacking.   'Corporate', on the Spanish
model, is closer, in the sense that most organisations representative of liberal-capitalist interests
are organically linked to the regime - which
probably established them and which probably puts its
own agents (perhaps retired army commanders) into
authority within them.   But the corporate image is
also misleading if it is taken to imply that the
principle form of linkage between state and citizens
is one based on alliances between broadly-defined
(and state -regulated) social groups.
Rather, the principle tie between citizens and
rulers is based on <u>cooption</u> of individuals and
private interests into a state-dominated decision-
making system, a 'technical' and supportive relationship which does not threaten the superior rationality
of state officials.[15]   There is of course bargaining
between state and private interests; but those who
control decision-making in the state are the ones who

decide who shall be admitted to the bargaining.
The great bulk of the population are excluded. With
this structure, the regime has been able to impose
modernisation from above, with scant regard for
democratic niceties or for bargaining with incorpor-
ative social groups.

We have seen this structure of cooption and
exclusion operating in the countryside.   The
farmers are comprehensively excluded from the
operations of the FLIA, not only in the sense that
their collective interests are not directly and
formally represented but also in the sense that they
feel unable even to exert influence, as individuals,
over those operations which affect them intimately.
And the recent 'reforms' which, under pressure from
above, SY FLIA was led to propose as a means of
furthering their 'Devotion to the service of farmers'
- a Suggestions Box, and opening the Field Stations
to farmers once a month from 13.00 to 18.00, for
instance - only show how far the farmers' exclusion
has been taken.   So does the reality of the SY
Public Newspaper.   On the other hand, there is an
elaborate and dense structure of cooption in the
form of the Hueng Non Gye leaders;   here indeed there
is some representational link, in that the Hueng Non
Gye leaders are nominated not by the FLIA but by the
village elders - though it must be remembered that the
the Hueng Non Gye leadership role is of little importance in the eyes of the regime, and the appointments
to what are seen as the important roles, the village
chief and the Saemaul Movement leader (in population
units often no bigger than 100 households), are
made from above, if often with informal local
'consultation'.

We have also seen how the structure of exclusion
and cooption is reinforced by the regime's intensive
promulgation of an ideology of anti-communism,
nationalism, and developmentalism, all personified
in the person of President Park.   The Saemaul
Movement is an important vehicle for the propagation
of this ideology in the countryside;   another is
the monthly meetings of the ban (sub-village units
of 14-20 households), for which each province
prepares a special newspaper; and we noted how the
senior-most officials of the FLIAs are receiving
training not in technical matters, like their
juniors, but in what is translated as 'Spiritual'
subjects.   Constant invocations of the threat from
the North and of the duty to serve the nation in
its development goals have served to check the
opposition of private entrepreneurs and dominant

groups, and so to facilitate implementation of
state policies. We have seen how farmers, talking
of their exclusion from influence in the FLIA, began
by criticising it and ended by saying that in the
light of the 'special security problem of Korea' it
was (almost) justified.

THE OPERATION OF BUREAUCRATIC HIERARCHIES

It is clear that in this context, with this
degree of state autonomy from multi-national capital,
national capital, and democratic bargaining, the
nature of the leadership's views and commitments are
of unusual significance in explaining the direction
of national economic development. But one has also
to consider how the bureaucracy itself operates.
For Jones and SaKong the main reason why state
intervention in South Korea has tended to promote
rather than impede development, in addition to the
firm leadership commitment to growth, is the rigid
enforcement of hierarchical command. Decisions at
one level of the hierarchy do result in the intended
change of behaviour at lower levels. 'Given the
dominant leadership commitment to growth, Ministers
prove themselves by the novelty and success of their
economic ideas. Similarly, subordinates prove their
worth within their ministry by conducting the staff
work necessary to generate and support their minister's
programs. The incentive system flowing from leadership commitment to growth thus permeates the hierarchy...' (1978, p. III-27). As between the bureaucracy and business, 'discretionary controls are
administered in such a way as not to seriously impede
the progress of business.... Economic growth under
private enterprise being well understood as the
dominant system goal, no official can afford to act
in a manner which obstructs that goal' (p. IV-76,
-77). [16]
Our study of SY FLIA suggests that the propensity to defer to hierarchical superiors is indeed
strong - stronger than in, say, the United States,
if such broad brush comparisons be allowed. This
propensity, reinforced by the common sense of
national purpose, heightens the susceptibility to
administrative guidance. A recent study [17] of
South Korean and Turkish bureaucrats throws some
more light on this susceptibility; 59 percent of
the South Koreans interviewed said that the most
important criterion in making decisions was the
views of their superiors, compared to only 17 percent of the Turks (many more of whom said "What I

think is best"), and on the significance of 'national
purpose', 58 percent of the South Koreans said
that the principle task of a civil servant is 'to
serve the nation as a whole', a reply given by only
11 percent of the Turks.   This helps to understand
why, although South Korean development plans seem to
be of an indicative kind only, once handed over to
the administration they in effect become binding on
officials to enforce.   The roots of this propensity
to defer to hierarchical superiors are deep in
Koreans' Confucian culture, which inculcates a
deference to authority whether based on age, education or position.   And that cultural tradition also
teaches that the government can do anything it sets
its mind to, based on 500 years of Confucian bureaucracy. [18]

But our study also suggests several ways in
which the notion of a rigidly authoritarian bureaucratic hierarchy needs careful qualification.   It
fails to give due weight to (1) the ways and
situations in which subordinate units within and
outside the bureaucracy attempt to defend themselves
from above; (2) what one might call groupishness,
or the willingness to merge one's identity within a
group, to take on its goals, apparently genuinely,
as one's own; (3) the normal style of authority
relations within face-to-face units of the bureaucracy and between officials and farmers in everyday
life.

When subordinate government officials are put
under intense and threatening pressure to meet
targets, they are very likely to falsify the
performance returns they send up the hierarchy if
they consider there is a reasonable chance of getting
away with it.   We noted earlier the results of a
study which found that township officials were reporting up the hierarchy that village HYV areas
were about 70 percent greater on average than the
heads of the same villages told the author of the
study.   Deception by township officials about the
number of new joint farms was very much greater.
Relatedly, we have seen that much of the data
available at SY FLIA about its environment,
physical structures, and water supply is highly
unreliable; and that because such data is not
checked from above the staff have little interest
in making it more reliable.   We have seen the
asymmetry in the care and attention given, on the
one hand, to collecting the information needed to
run the irrigation system effectively and at least
cost, and on the other, to collecting and presenting

and if expedient falsifying the information wanted
by the central government.   These points suggest
that judgements on how effective the government's
interventions have actually been in modifying
behaviour may be difficult because of biases in the
indicators of achievement - the result of people at
lower levels of the hierarchy protecting themselves
against punitive sanctions for underperformance.
However, both this specific problem and the wider
problem (as seen from the top) of compliance within
the government apparatus may be greater in the rural
than in the urban-industrial context, because more
of the central government's 'arms and legs' in the
countryside than in the cities are parastatal agencies
such as the FLIAs and the NACF.   One might expect
they would be more disposed than direct extensions
of the central government hierarchies to defend
themselves from scrutiny from above.

The second and third qualifications - groupishness and the normal style of authority relations -
are closely related. [19]   In the microcosm of SY
FLIA we have seen that the sense of the FLIA as a
community, the sense of prideful attachment to it,
is promoted by several features of work organisation:

- lifetime employment expectations in the one
  organisation;

- the senior officials (other than the
  President) are promotees, and see themselves
  rather as elders of a community;

- relatively heavy weight to length of service
  in the determination of salary, to compensate
  those who fail to rise up in the narrow rank
  ladders;

- organisation of work on a group basis (for
  example, the submission and review of weekly
  section work plans).

We have also seen how the perceived need for defence
from higher scrutiny helps to maintain the sense of
community.

We remarked, too, on the absence of wide
disparities of income, of obvious differences in
class culture, in speech, dress, or bearing;   the
absence of rank-related segregation of facilities
(like toilets, canteens);   the absence of arrogance
and aloofness, of domineering bluster in the exercise
of authority in face-to-face relations - on the
contrary, the quiet style of authority (which for
all the reality of hierarchy and deference makes use
of the adjective 'authoritarian' to describe it

problematic); and we remarked on the strength of an
informal egalitarian ethic in social relations, coexist-
ing in complex ways with a formal hierarchical ethic.

It makes good sense to suppose that this quiet style
of authority and groupishness reinforce each other.
The propensity to merge one's identity within a group is
likely to be greater where authority relations within
the group are softened in this way, and authority
relations can be quieter yet still effective where there
is a more open-ended merging of individuals with the group.

Just how the sense of groupishness in parts of the
state apparatus affects the performance of those parts and
of the larger hierarchy is difficult to specify. One
might make the following points:

(1) If SY FLIA is at all typical, the sense of
groupishness helps to defend the unit from scrutiny and
control from above, by promoting employees' identification with the unit as against the higher authorities.

(2) Within the unit it promotes subordinates'
identification with and deference to organisational
superiors, and reduces the likelihood that such resentments as do arise will lead to concerted action. Hence
it probably makes more effective the carrying out of
orders which come from inside the organisation. The
monthly meeting of all staff, which is one of the
institutional devices for promoting the sense of community,
illustrates that subordinates are seen as implementors of
orders from above rather than as potential contributors
of useful ideas and information; but their collective
identification with the FLIA makes this more acceptable
than it might otherwise be.

We noted in SY FLIA - and similar observations have
been made in central government ministries below the
topmost levels [20] - an approximately inverse correlation
between hierarchical position and work effort. This is
surprising, in view of a popular image of Korean bureaucrats as exemplars of military-like efficiency and
discipline - an image used by Jones and SaKong in their
remark that 'government policy response to changing
conditions is typically closer to the alacrity of a crack
air force unit scrambling to the attack than to the
lethargy usually associated with bureaucracy' (1978, p.IX
-7). This may apply at the top levels of government
ministries in Seoul; but amongst the managers of SY FLIA,
at least, there was no sign of such qualities, no sign of
'a nagging inner urge (to work) that leaves one uncomfortable at the nonfulfillment of duty if one denies it', as
the work ethic has been defined. [21] Such absence may
indicate less a general characteristic of South Korean
bureaucracy than a characteristic of those governmental
organisations whose tasks are largely matters of routine

rather than responding to a constantly changing environment. And insofar as the reason is cultural, as well as structural, it may reflect a Korean (and Japanese) [22] expectation of rank relations which is different to that prevailing in the West; it is, according to this expectation, not necessary for the top man with the top pay to take the top burden of decision-making - it is enough that he facilitate the working together of his subordinates and take responsibility if things go wrong. In any case, the SY material suggests one should regard with caution any sweeping assumption of 'leadership by the example of hard work' in the South Korean bureaucracy.

(3) The collective concern with pressures from above, coupled with the exclusion of farmers not only from the FLIA but from all government administration, means that the performance of the main services to farmers can be carried out in a routine and unconcerned way - except when there is a crisis, as in a severe drought or bad pest attack. Because farmers have no way of bringing complaints to bear on the FLIA in any concerted way, or of by-passing the FLIA to get pressure brought on it from higher up the hierarchy, so one finds, for example, reservoirs without railings on the walkways from the shore to the offtake structures - despite local farmers' concern at the danger this poses for young children. The failure of staff to be concerned about improving the operating procedures and information of the irrigation system except through expensive engineering changes (the charges for which are passed on to farmers) is another result of the same set of influences.

(4) We can extend the discussion of the impact of groupishness and the style of superior and subordinate relations to relations between officials and farmers. While earlier we emphasised the exclusionary character of the regime, it has also to be emphasised that the exclusion is maintained not only by the judicious cooption of state-designated interest leaders but also, in the countryside, by a government presence so dense that contact between officials and farmers is frequent, and is often softened by the same quietness of style, and by the same informal egalitarian ethic, as we noted within the bureaucracy. Contact between FLIA staff and farmers is normally between individuals, not groups - typically it is between a few farmers walking to their fields along the canal bank and a FLIA staff member who passes en route to check on the patroller. In this context, the contact is normally guided by the informal egalitarian ethic rather than the formal hierarchical ethic, and is strikingly different, in its assumption of an underlying equality of condition between farmers and staff, to relations between irrigation officials and farmers in India. Not only is there no assumption that authority

to be effective must be aloof and domineering; there is little cultural difference between them. One would not find in India, as one might in South Korea, irrigation officers getting down into an irrigation channel alongside the patroller and farmers to help clear a blockage or move the water along in a drought. To the extent that such social relations are common in local government-farmer contact, the effect is to personalise the power structure of the regime and make it seem non-bureaucratic; which makes it more difficult for farmers to perceive general 'issues' and raise generalised complaints as distinct from individual or village 'problems'. Moreover, on the one matter which irrigators do perceive as a general 'issue', namely water charges, the staff of SY FLIA are responsive, to the extent that they were distinctly reluctant to contemplate increasing water charges for fear of farmers' discontent (though this did not lead them to search for cheaper alternatives to a pump station as a means of improving water supply in the tail-end Section referred to in Chapter 4). If the matter is one about which large numbers of irrigators are concerned and apprehensive, some 'interest aggregation' can take place through this structure of personalised relations between staff and farmers.

When the full force of the regime's coercive power is to be turned on the farmers, then the sense of groupness within the bureaucratic unit facilitates implementation of the orders. When there is little by way of cultural difference between officials and farmers to validate such action (as there commonly is in India), then some collective support is clearly desirable for those whose job it is, for example, to forcibly remove the old farmhouse roofs (so that the farmers have to replace them with roofs to Saemaul specifications), or to forcibly remove the farmers' seed and replace it with the government-favoured variety.

Just what these points add up to in terms of their net impact on the effectiveness of the public bureaucracy is not easy to say. They do however suggest that the enforcement of hierarchical command may be a good deal less rigid than Jones and SaKong imply, at least in some parts of the bureaucracy. The danger of the 'rigid hierarchy' image (and the more generic notion of the 'hard' state) is that it leads too easily to the assumption that the state is so powerful that attention can properly be restricted to the various techniques of implementation it uses, taking for granted that the attempt at control from above is successful. Our examination of SY FLIA suggests a degree of autonomy of parts of the bureaucracy which one might not expect from a macro perspective, for the coherence of the state seems greater at the top than it does at the base.

THE FUTURE OF THE DIRECTIVE STATE

But in relation to most other Third World
countries, the bureaucratic hierarchy is undoubtedly
relatively rigid in Jones and SaKong's sense, and this,
coupled with the leadership commitment to growth, is
undoubtedly an important element amongst the 'internal'
causes of South Korea's rapid growth.   Yet research on
how bureaucratic hierarchies operate in the Korean context
is remarkably thin, considering how central the role of
the state has been in directing that growth.
This lacuna is by no means special to South Korean
studies.   At the same time as the role of the modern
state has grown dramatically in the underdeveloped world,
political and economic theory continues to overlook it.
The recent reassertion of a neo-classical development
orthodoxy, using South Korean and Taiwan as living
demonstrations of its soundness, tends positively to
occlude our perception of that role.   In future,
especially during periods of prolonged world economic
stagnation, this role is likely to become even more
important.   Highly authoritarian states with very
limited democratic institutions are likely to have
competitive advantages over more democratic states, by
virtue of being able to direct the utilisation of huge
amounts of investible resources while social unrest
worsens the investment climate in more democratic countries.
The authoritarian states may be able to keep their
productivity driving forward faster than the latter.
Yet the risks of such states are also high.   We noted
earlier some of the likely counter-productive effects of
the South Korean government's strenuous efforts to compel
and induce higher agricultural productivity.   It can
plausibly be argued that to lock up as much as 75-80
percent of new equipment investment in long gestation
heavy industrial projects at a time of massive excess
capacity in those sectors world-wide has been a serious
miscalculation, which could only be acted on because the
state controls so much of the economy's investment fund.
The very methods that are used to rule can also undermine
the government's workable authority.   The 200,000 people
of the southern city and province of Kwangju who in
May 1980 rose up against the central government, for a
week overturning its writ, were protesting against being
made the object of commands and obligations from their
strong and exclusionary government. [23]   We have seen how
people in the bureaucratic hierarchy routinely attempt to
evade or lessen the pressures of control from above.
And there is no doubt that the private industrial sector
in South Korea is pressing the government to slacken its
controls.   Farmers too can be expected to express more
open criticism of government direction, as they gain more
of the assertiveness which wealth and education tends to

confer.   On the other hand, it is also clear that to
Korean administrators, heirs to 500 years of Confucian
bureaucracy, the market forces wanted by the private
sector look like anarchy in which no faith should be
placed.   The future of the tighly directive role of
the state is then bound to be contested, especially if
the regime ceases to be seen as effective - if economic
growth stops and/or the distribution of benefits ceases
to trickle down.

The present study has shown, I hope, the utility for
discovering and elucidating the complexities of the state's
role of - in Mills' words (p.1) - moving grandly at the
macroscopic level and minutely at the microscopic level,
shuttling between levels in instituting the problem and
in explaining it.

NOTES

1. For references to examples from these two bodies
of literature, see Chapter 1, n. 2 and 6.
2. See Little 1979, p. 34, 35.   One should add as
a further condition, exporters' confidence that the
government would be able to implement and stick to these
policies.
3. I am indebted to discussions with Manfred
Bienefeld in formulating this argument.
4. In addition to the neo-classical writers on South
Korea, see Mellor 1976, Chp. 11 ('Planning and the strategy
for growth') for another example of a growth strategy
formulated with only casual attention to the changing
international context of national development.
5. Hong 1980, p. 33.
6. See Jones and SaKong 1978.
7. See United States, National Foreign Assessment
Centre 1978.
8. Michell 1980.   The Fourth Five Year Plan states
as an explicit objective the elimination of all foreign
savings by 1981.   Foreign savings is not defined, but
presumably includes all foreign direct investment plus
all loans for investment projects.   The objective has
been turned on its head in 1980.
9. Michell 1980.   On North Korea's _juche_, see
White 1975.
10. See Luedde-Neurath 1980.   I have emphasised the
role of the state in explaining why capital flows from
outside did not have the distorting, blocking effects
predicted by dependency theory.   But the relative strength,
self-confidence and national orientation of the industrial
bourgeoisie is another, partly independent causal factor.
The causes of this factor have been little researched.
11. See Jones and SaKong 1978.
12. Korea Exchange Bank 1980.   I thank Richard Luedde-
Neurath for this reference.

13. See Datta-Chaudhuri 1979.
14. Griffin 1979, p. 375-6.
15. I draw here on the useful analysis of Cardoso 1979.
16. Note however that in contrast to the classic totalitarian regimes of Hitler's Germany and Stalin's Russia, the Park regime, whether because it is not strong enough or has not wished to, has not seriously tried either in the governmental bureaucracy or in the society at large to make people say the things it approves of. It has used its repressive apparatus to try to ensure that people do not say things it does not approve of - in particular, criticism of President Park himself or anything complimentary to North Korea.
17. Heper et al. 1980.
18. Michell 1980.
19. My discussion of groupishness and the style of authority is indebted to Dore 1981.
20. Chapter 6, n.8.
21. Dore 1973, p. 245.
22. Dore 1981.
23. Student dissatisfaction over the slow progress in plans to return to civilian and democratic rule after the assassination of President Park in late 1979 came into the open in March 1980, and was especially strongly expressed in Kwangju, home of the powerful dissident leader Kim Dae Jung. The jailing of Kim for persistent criticism of the regime gave further impetus to the protest. Martial law was declared in May, many politicians students, labour leaders and civil rights leaders were arrested throughout the country. An angry protest at Kwangju's university was put down with such brutality as to bring thousands of protesting civilians onto the streets. The protest spread with remarkable momentum, and government control in the city and surrounding towns was effectively overturned. See Financial Times, 20-25 May 1980, various articles.

Bibliography

Abel, M., 1975, 'Irrigation systems in Taiwan: management
     of a decentralised public enterprise', Staff Papers
     Series, July, Department of Agricultural and Applied
     Economics, University of Minnesota, Institute of
     Agriculture, St. Paul, Minnesota.
Acqua, R., 1974, Local Institutions and Rural Development
     in South Korea. Cornell University, Special Series
     on Rural Local Government.
Adelman, I. and S. Robinson, 1978, Income Distribution
     Policy in Developing Countries: A Case Study of
     Korea. Published for the World Bank by Oxford
     University Press.
Amin, S., 1974, Accumulation on a World Scale: A
     Critique of the Theory of Underdevelopment. Monthly
     Review Press, New York.
Amnesty International, 1977, Report of an Amnesty Inter-
     national Mission to the Republic of Korea, 27 March -
     9 April 1975. Amnesty International Publications,
     London.
___, 1979, Ali Lameda: A Personal Account of the Exper-
     ience of a Prisoner of Conscience in the Democratic
     People' Republic of Korea. Amnesty International
     Secretariate, London.
Apthorpe, R., 1979, 'The burden of land reform in Taiwan:
     an Asian model land reform re-analysed', World
     Development 7 (4/5), pp. 519-530.
Asian Development Bank, 1979, Key Indicators of Developing
     Member Countries. Bangkok, October.
Bae-ho Hahn, 1975, 'The authority structure of Korean
     politics', in Korean Politics in Transition, (ed.)
     E. Reynolds, University of Washington Press.
Bai Moo Ki, 1978, 'Examining Adelman's view on relative
     income equity in Korea: with focus on her studies
     outlined in the World Bank Report', Social Science
     Journal (The Korean Social Science Research Council),
     Vol. 5, No. 1, pp. 85-99.
Ban, S., 1977, 'Growth and Sources of Agricultural Prod-
     uction and Productivity in Korea 1945-1974', Korea
     Modernisation Study Series (3),Working Paper 7706,
     Korea Development Institute, Seoul.
Bennett, J., 1974, 'Anthropological contributions to the
     cultural ecology and management of water resources',
     in Man and Water - the Social Sciences in Manage-
     ment of Water Resources, (ed.) L. Douglas James,
     University of Kentucky Press.
Bergsman, J., 1980, 'Growth: a tale of two nations -
     Korea', News and View from the World Bank, May-June,
     Washington, D.C., pp. 1-4.
Bienefeld, M., 1980, 'Dependency in the eighties',
     Bulletin, Vol. 12, No. 1, Institute of Development
     Studies, Sussex.
Bienefeld, M. and M. Godfrey, eds., forthcoming, The
     Struggle for Development: National Strategies in an

International Context. John Wiley, Chichester.

Bottrall, A., 1978, 'Technology and management in irrigated agriculture', Overseas Development Institute's Review, No. 2, pp. 22-50.

Brandt Commission (Independent Commission on International Issues), 1980, North-South: A Programme for Survival. Pan Books, London.

Brandt, V., 1971, A Korean Village Between Farm and Sea. Harvard University Press.

___, 1977, 'Why rural Korea was transformed', The Asia Wall Street Journal, Jan. 14.

Brandt, V. and Man-gap Lee, 1977, Community Development Program in Korea. Korea National Commission for UNESCO, May, Seoul.

Brenner, R., 1977, 'The origins of capitalist development: a critique of neo-Smithian Marxism', New Left Review, No. 104, July/August, pp. 25-92.

Brown, G., 1973, Korean Pricing Policies and Economic Development in the 1960s. Johns Hopkins Press, Baltimore.

C.W. Thornthwaite Associates, 1963, Average Climatic Water Balance Data of the Continents, Part II. Centerton, New Jersey.

Cardoso, F., 1979, 'On the characterisation of authoritarian regimes in Latin America', in (ed.) D. Collier, The New Authoritarianism in Latin America, Princeton University Press.

Cho, Suk-Choon, 1975, 'The bureaucracy', in E. Wright (ed.) Korean Politics in Transition. University of Washington Press.

Cole, D. and P. Lyman, 1971, Korean Development: The Interplay of Politics and Economics. Harvard University Press.

Colombo, U., D. Johnson, T. Shishido, 1977, Reducing Malnutrition in Developing Countries: Increasing Rice Production in South and Southeast Asia. Report of the Trilateral North-South Food Task Force to the Trilateral Commission. The Trilateral Commission, New York.

Coward, E.W., 1976, 'Indigenous organisation, bureaucracy and development: the case of irrigation', J. Development Studies, 13(1), pp. 92-105.

Critchfield, H., 1966, General Climatology. 2nd ed., Prentice--Hall, New Jersey.

Crosson, P., 1975, 'Institutional obstacles to expansion of world food production', Science, Vol. 188, No. 4188, 9 May, pp. 519-524.

Cumings, B., 1974, 'Kim's Korean Communism', Problems of Communism, XXIII, March-April.

Cumings, B., 1974a, 'Is Korea a mass society?', in Occasional Papers on Korea, No. 1, April. Edited by J. Palais. The Joint Committee on Korean Studies of the American Council of Learned Societies and the Social Science Research Council.

Dahl, R. and C. Lindblom, 1953, Politics, Economics and Welfare: Planning and Politic-Economic Processes Resolved into Basic Social Processes. Harper, New York.

Datta-Chaudhuri, M., 1979, 'Industrialisation and foreign trade: an analysis based on the development experiences of the Republic of Korea and the Philippines', Asian Employment Programme Working Papers, Asian Regional Team for Employment Promotion (ARTEP), International Labour Organisation, Bangkok.

Diaz-Alejandro, C., 1978, 'Delinking North and South: Unshackled or Unhinged', in Rich and Poor Nations in the World Economy, (eds.) A. Fishlow, C. Diaz-Alejandro, R. Fagen, R. Marsen, 1980s Project/Council on Foreign Relations, McGraw-Hill, New York.

Dore, R., 1973, English Factory - Japanese Factory: The Origins of National Diversity in Industrial Relations. Allen and Unwin, London.

Dore, R., 1981, 'Individualism East and West, Then and Now', unpublished manuscript, Institute of Development Studies.

Easey, W. and G. McCormack, 1977, 'South Korean society: the deepening nightmare', in McCormack and Gittings (eds.).

Eyre, J.D., 1955, 'Water controls in a Japanese irrigation system', The Geographical Review, XLV (2), 197-216.

Financial Times, 1979, 'Financial Times Survey: South Korea', 2 April, London.

____, 1979a, 'Financial Times Survey: South Korea', June 9, London.

____, 1980, various articles on the Kwangju uprising, 20-25 May.

Food and Agriculture Organisation (FAO), 1978, Fertiliser Yearbook 1978. Rome.

____, 1980, Monthly Bulletin of Statistics, January. Rome.

Foster-Carter, A., 1977, 'North Korea: Development and self-reliance, a critical appraisal', Bulletin of Concerned Asian Scholars, IX(1), Jan-Mar, pp. 45-57.

Frank, A., 1976, 'Multilateral merchandise trade imbalances and uneven economic development', The Journal of European Economic History, Vol. 5, No. 2.

French, J. and P. Lyman, 1970, Political Results of Land Reforms. USAID Spring Review of Land Reform, Analytical Papers, Washington, D.C.

Griffin, K. with the assistance of A.Ghose, 1979, 'Growth and impoverishment in the rural areas of Asia', World Development, Vol. 7, No. 4/5.

Hasan, P., 1976, Korea, Problems and Issues in a Rapidly Growing Economy. Published for the World Bank, Johns Hopkins University Press.

Hayami, Y. and V. Ruttan, 1971, Agricultural Development: An International Perspective. Johns Hopkins University Press.

164

Heginbotham, S., 1975, Cultures in Conflict: The Four
Faces of Indian Bureaucracy . Colombia University
Press.
Henderson, G., 1968, Korea: The Politics of the Vortex.
Harvard University Press.
Heper, M., Chong Lim Kim, and Seong-Tong Pai, 1980, 'The
role of bureaucracy and regime types: a comparative
study of Turkish and South Korean higher civil
servants', Administration and Society, Vol. 12, No.2.
Hong, Wong Tack, 1980, 'Trade, industrial growth, and
income distribution in Korea', unpublished manuscript,
Institute of Development Studies.
Hunt, R. and E. Hunt, 1976, 'Canal irrigation and local
social organisation', Current Anthropology, Vol. 17,
No. 3, pp. 389-411.
Ishikawa, S., 1967, Economic Development in Asian
Perspective , Economic Research Series No. 8, The
Institute of Economic Research, Hitotsubashi
University.
Ishikawa, S., 1978, Labour Absorption in Asian Agriculture.
Asian Regional Programme for Employment Promotion,
International Labour Organisation, Bangkok.
Jones, L. and Il SaKong, 1978, Government and Entre-
preneurship in Economic Development: The Korean
Case . Korea Modernisation Study Series (10),
Working Paper 7802, Korea Development Institute,
Seoul.
Kim, Chang Soo, 1977, 'Marginalisation, development and
the Korean workers' movement', Ampo, 9(3), pp.20-39.
Kim, Dong-il, 1980, 'A preliminary profile of Korean
farmers and their villages', Appendix E in Steinberg
et al.
Kim, Sung-Hoon, 1978, 'The successful drought counter-
measures in Korean agriculture', Asian Economies,
No. 24, March, Research Institute of Asian Economies,
Seoul, Republic of Korea.
Korea Annual 1979. Hapdong News Agency, Seoul.
Korea Exchange Bank, 1980, 'Adjustment of Korea's heavy
and chemical industry investment', Monthly Review
Vol. XIV, No. 12.
Korea, Republic of, Bureau of Statistics, 1979, Monthly
Statistics of Korea, Seoul.
___, Economic Planning Board, 1979, Major Statistics of
Korean Economy, 1979. Seoul.
___, Ministry of Agriculture and Fisheries (MAF), 1977,
Statistical Yearbook. Seoul.
___, MAF, 1978, Yearbook of Agricultural and Forestry
Statistics, 1977. Seoul.
___, 1978a, Report on the Results of Farm Household Economy
Survey. Seoul.
___, MAF, Agricultural Development Corporation, 1972,
National Seminar on Water Management at the Farm
Level, Proceedings. Seoul.

___, MAF, Agricultural Development Corporation, 1976, 'Post Evaluation report on small and medium scale irrigation projects sponsored by USAID, Interim Report', December.

___, MAF, Agricultural Development Corporation, 1978, Yearbook of Land and Water Development Statistics, Seoul.

___, MAF, FLIA Management Bureau, 1978, 'FLIAs independently promote improvements', mimeo, Seoul.

___, Ministry of Home Affairs, 1972, Local Government in Korea. Seoul.

___, National Agricultural Cooperative Federation (NACF), 1977, Annual Report. Seoul.

Kuznets, P., 1977, Economic Growth and Structure in the Republic of Korea. Yale University Press.

Lee, E., 1979, 'Egalitarian peasant farming and rural development: the case of South Korea', World Development 7, pp. 493-517.

Lee, Man Gap, 1978, 'A river to be crossed: overcoming the sense of relative deprivation', Korea Journal, Vol. 18, No. 8, Korea National Commission for UNESCO.

Lees, S., 1974, 'Hydraulic development as a process of response', Human Ecology, Vol. 2, No. 3, pp. 159-175.

Leonard, D., 1977, Reaching the Peasant Farmer: Organisational Theory and Practice in Kenya. University of Chicago Press.

Levine, G., 1977, 'Sub-utilisation of irrigation systems: a perspective for viewing the problem', paper presented at the Seminar on Sub-utilisation of Irrigation Systems in Tropical Latin America, 23-27 May, CIDIAT, Merida, Venezuela.

---, 1977a, 'Management components in irrigation system design and operation', Agricultural Administration, Vol. 4, No. 1, January.

---, 1979, 'Hardware and software: an engineering perspective on the mix for irrigation management', paper presented at workshop on Irrigation Research, International Rice Research Institute, Los Banos, Philippines, 26-30 March.

---, 1979a, 'Water use and water management - tradeoff implications for water efficiency', paper presented at the IFPRI-IRRI-IFDC Symposium on Rice Policy, Los Banos, Philippines, May.

Levine, G., L. Chin, S. Miranda, 1976, 'Requirements for the successful introduction and management of rotational irrigation', Agricultural Water Management, 1, 41-56.

Little, I., 1979, 'The experience and causes of rapid labour-intensive development in Korea, Taiwan, Hong Kong, and Singapore; and the possibilities of emulation', Asian Employment Programme Working Papers, Asian Regional Team for Employment Promotion, International Labour Organisation, Bangkok.

Long, D., 1977, 'Repression and development in the periphery:
    South Korea', Bulletin of Concerned Asian Scholars,
    Vol. 9, No. 2, pp. 26-41.
Luedde-Neurath, R., 1980, 'Export orientation in South
    Korea: How helpful is dependency thinking to its
    analysis?', Bulletin, Vol. 12, No. 1, Institute
    of Development Studies, Sussex.
McCormack, G., 1977, 'The South Korean economy: GNP
    versus the people', in McCormack and Gittings (eds.).
McCormack G. and J. Gittings (eds.), 1977, Crisis in Korea.
    Produced by the Korea Committee, London and the
    Transnational Institute. Published by the Bertrand
    Russell Peace Foundation Ltd., Nottingham, for
    Spokesman Books.
Marx, K., 1964, Pre-capitalist Economic Formations. With
    an introduction by E. Hobsbawm. Lawrence and Wishart,
    London.
Mellor, J., 1976, The New Economics of Growth: A Strategy
    for India and the Developing World. Cornell University
    Press.
Michell, A., 1980, 'South Korea: the first country to go
    from LDC to industrial nation in one generation?',
    unpublished manuscript, University of Hull. Revised
    version in Bienefeld and Godfrey (eds.).
Mills, C.W., 1963, 'Two styles of social science research'.
    In Power, Politics and People, (ed.) I. Horowitz,
    Oxford University Press.
Mitchell, W., 1973, 'The hydraulic hypothesis: a reappraisal',
    Current Anthropology, Vol. 14, No. 5, pp. 532-534.
Moon, P. and B. Ryu, 1977, 'Korea's agricultural policies
    in historical perspective', Working Paper Series, No.
    7704, Korea Development Institute, Seoul.
Moore, M. 1980, 'The management of irrigation systems in
    Sri Lanka: a study in practical sociology', Sri
    Lanka Journal of Social Sciences, 2 (2).
Myrdal, G., 1968, Asian Drama, An Inquiry into the
    Poverty of Nations. 3 vols. Penguin Books, Harmonds-
    worth.
Oh, Ho-Sung, 1978, 'Customary rules of water management
    for small irrigation reservoirs in Korea', J. Rural
    Development, 1(1), Nov., Korea Rural Economics
    Institute, Seoul.
Pak, Ki-Hyuk, and S. Gamble, 1975, The Changing Korean
    Village. Shin-hung Press, Seoul.
Pak, Ki Sung, n.d. (1959-60), Significance of Korean
    Irrigation. Bureau of Farmland Management, Ministry
    of Agriculture, Republic of Korea.
Park, Chung Hee, 1962, Our Nation's Path: Ideology of
    Social Reconstruction. Dong-A Publishing Co., Seoul.
Park, Chung Hee, 1979, Korea Reborn: A Model for Develop-
    ment. Prentice-Hall, New Jersey.
Park Ung Suh, 1978, 'Modern economic development in the
    Republic of Korea', The Seoul National University
    Economic Review, 12(1).

Pasternak, B., 1968, 'Social consequences of equalising
    irrigation access', Human Organisation, Vol. 27, No.
    4, pp. 332-343.
Pereira, C., A. Aboukhaled, A. Felleke, D. Hillel, A.
    Moursi, 1979, Opportunities for Increase of World
    Food Production from the Irrigated Lands of
    Developing countries. Report to the Technical
    Advisory Committee of the Consultative Group on
    International Agricultural Research. International
    Development Research Council, Ottawa, April.
Rao, D., 1978, 'Economic growth and equity in the Republic
    of Korea', World Development, 6(3), pp. 383-396.
Reed, E., 1979, Group Farming in Smallholder Agriculture:
    Experience and Potential in South Korea. Unpublished
    Ph. D. thesis, University of Wisconsin-Madison.
Richardson, R., 1979, 'Rising cost of self-sufficiency',
    Far Eastern Economic Review, 8 June, pp. 84-7.
Ryu, Han Yeal, 1972, 'How to save irrigation water in
    cultivation of rice', in MAF, Agricultural Develop-
    ment Corporation.
Sawada, S., 1972, 'The development of rice productivity
    in Japan', in Agriculture and Economic Development,
    (ed.) Japan Economic Research Centre, Tokyo, Vol. 1.
Steinberg, D., 1980, 'Change, local government, and
    rural participation in Korean rural development',
    Appendix G in Steinberg et al.
___, 1980a, 'Donor experience in irrigation in Korea: The
    IBRD example', Appendix H in Steinberg et al.
Steinberg, D., R. Morrow, I. Palmer, Kim Dong-il, 1980,
    Korean Irrigation. Project Impact Evaluation Report.
    United States Agency for International Development
    (USAID), September, mimeo.
Thornthwaite, C., and J. Mather, 1955, 'The water budget
    and its uses in irrigation', in Water, 1955 Yearbook
    of Agriculture, Washington, Government Printing
    Office.
UNDP/FAO, 1974, Upland Development and Watershed Manage-
    ment: Republic of Korea, Comprehensive Technical
    Report. Rome.
United States, National Foreign Assessment Centre, 1978,
    'Korea: the economic race between the North and the
    South', Washington D.C.
Vandermeer, C., 1968, 'Changing water control in a Taiwan-
    ese rice-field irrigation system', Ann. Assn. Amer.
    Geog. 58, pp. 720-747.
Wade, L. and Kim Bong Sik, 1977, The Political Economy of
    Success: Public Policy and Economic Development in the
    Republic of Korea. Hyung Hee University Press,
    Seoul.
Wade, R.H., 1979, 'The social response to irrigated
    agriculture: an Indian case study', Journal of
    Development Studies, 16(1), pp. 3-26.
___, 1980, Irrigation potential and performance: man

    mismanagement under South Indian canals', mimeo,
Institute of Development Studies.

___, forthcoming, Irrigation Potential and Performance:
Man Mismanagement Under South Indian Canals (tent-
ative title).

Wade, R.H. and R. Chambers, 1980, 'Managing the main system:
canal irrigation's blind spot', Economic and
Political Weekly, Vol. XV, No. 39, Review of
Agriculture, September, pp. A-107-112.

Wallerstein, I., 1974, 'Dependence in an inter-dependent
world: the limited possibilities of change in the
capitalist world-economy', African Studies Review,
No. 1, pp. 1-26.

Wen, L.J., 1977, 'China, Republic of', in Farm Water
Management for Rice Cultivation. Asian Productivity
Organisation, Tokyo.

Westphal, L., 1978, 'The Republic of Korea's experience
with export-led industrial development', World
Development 6(3), pp. 347-382.

White, G., 1975, 'North Korean chuch'e: the political
economy of independence', Bulletin of Concerned
Asian Scholars, April-June.

Wittfogel, K., 1963 (1957), Oriental Despotism, A
Comparative Study of Total Power. Yale University
Press.

Wook Dong Han, 1972, 'Application of groundwater and its
cold water damage to rice', in MAF,Agricultural
Development Corporation, 1972.

World Bank, 1973, Agricultural Sector Survey, Republic of
Korea. 4 volumes, Washington D.C.

World Bank, 1978, World Development Report, 1978.
Washington DC.

Young Whan Kihl, 1979, 'Politics and agrarian change in
South Korea: rural modernisation by "induced"
mobilisation', in Food, Politics, and Agricultural
Development, (eds) R. Hopkins, D. Puchala, and
R. Talbot, Westview Press, Colorado.

Index